T0355824

GIFTS *of* GRIEF

A Man's Revelations
After Sudden Loss

JACOB WATSON

BALBOA.PRESS
A DIVISION OF HAY HOUSE

Balboa Press books may be ordered through booksellers or by contacting:

Balboa Press
A Division of Hay House
1663 Liberty Drive
Bloomington, IN 47403
www.balboapress.com
844-682-1282

Print information available on the last page.

ISBN: 979-8-7652-5522-3 (sc)
ISBN: 979-8-7652-5521-6 (e)

Library of Congress Control Number: 2024918332

Balboa Press rev. date: 08/30/2024

Praise

The radiant discovery that is the treasure hidden at the heart of heartbreak and loss illumines Jacob Watson's humble, tender, and finely written exploration of the gifts that came after the death of his wife of many years. Read this beautiful and noble book slowly and integrate its message to bring you hope and peace in a darkening world.

—Andrew Harvey, coauthor of *Radical Regeneration*

Gifts of Grief is a gift to all—not only those who experience the loss of a partner but all those in long-term relationships. Jacob describes who he was in a partnership and then who he finds himself to be on his own. He speaks of feeling supported by his wife from the spirit world. Though Jacob is a minister, his book never preaches; instead he shares his moment-to-moment experience of grief as a sorrow and as a gift.

—Rev. Joel Grossman, cohost of the *Lifting Your Spirit* podcast, and Northern New England director of spiritual services, Constellation Hospice

With brutal honesty and breathtaking vulnerability, Watson explores his journey with grief after the sudden untimely death of his beloved wife. He reminds us that even in our darkest hours we are given gifts of wisdom, understanding, and strength if we are open and receptive enough to receive and recognize them.

—Rev. Priscilla Platt, end-of-life consultant

Gifts of Grief is a remarkable and sacred transmission of the gifts and spiritual teachings that arose phoenixlike out of the ashes of the sudden and brutal loss of his dear Kristine. Jacob is a master teacher, and the teachings here are important and healing to all those of us who experience loss and grief. That would be 100 percent of us!

—Ron Feintech, licensed psychologist and practitioner of integrative Buddhism

What I love about this book is that you don't actually read it; you experience it alongside the author. Jacob Watson takes us by the hand and, with humility, rawness, and authenticity, allows us to witness the unedited sounds of a bruised and shattered heart. He shows us that when we express the brokenness of grief, the gifts walk alongside it. I will recommend this gem to grieving others as a gift … until they find their own.

—Phyllida Anam-Áire, Irish psychotherapist, author of *The Last Ecstasy of Life*, and singer with nine CDs

Jacob Watson's book *Gifts of Grief: A Man's Revelations after Sudden Loss* is an intimate, poetic meditation on the author's spiritual development following the death of his wife, Kristine. The book is a love story; each chapter begins with a love note from Kristine to Jacob written over the course of their thirty-five-year marriage. Watson takes the reader along with him as he describes his deep, undying love for his wife, and the shock and disbelief that followed her sudden death. Perhaps most poignantly, Watson skillfully captures his transformative awakening to the joyful celebration of his own single, separate self.

—Robert Zucker, author of *The Journey through Grief and Loss: Helping Yourself and Your Child When Grief Is Shared*

Gifts of Grief is a poignant and deeply profound memoir. From his career in grief counseling and his roles starting the Center for Grieving Children and the interfaith Chaplaincy Institute of Maine, Jacob offers a unique perspective as a spiritual leader navigating the complexities of personal loss. His expertise, grace, and wisdom shine through as he eloquently articulates the eternal presence of love and the divine. This beautiful book is a treasure guide, offering a path to freedom.

—Alison Caswell, LCPC psychotherapist

In his book *Gifts of Grief*, Jacob Watson shares his courageous journey with deep grief. Think of crossing a flowing stream by carefully stepping on a series of stones, as Jacob in artful and intensely personal chapters guides the reader from one shore to another. Jacob states, "I could trust my grief and its processes"—an insight that proves a steady, compassionate, and trustworthy companion.

—Rev. Tom Kircher, interfaith minister, chaplain for Seafarer's Friend

Jacob's book is personal and immediate, very accessible and readable. I'm drawn in right away, and I empathically feel his process. He doesn't shrink from the pain of his loss but frames it in terms of gifts. The love letters in the beginning of each chapter really work. *Gifts of Grief* is a real gift.

—Leah Chyten, author of *Light Radiance Splendor* and *Soul of the Mountain*

Jacob's book is a true expression of a heart full of love and grief after a sudden death. The hope shared after the deep pain of loss has impacted many in Maine and beyond.

—Anne Heros, former executive director, Center for Grieving Children

To Kristine, my dear partner, who gave me over thirty-five years of tender and passionate love; my life here is forever blessed.

To my four children and their partners, who loved me through my grief.

He was a man of sorrow, and acquainted with grief.
　　　　　　　　　　　　　　—Handel's Messiah

What's lost is nothing to what's found, and all the death that ever was, set next to life, would scarcely fill a cup.
　　　　　　　　　　　　　　—Frederick Buechner

Contents

Preface

This book began as a journal to survive Kristine's sudden death. Nothing can change the fact that Kristine was in my life for almost forty years. We had been married for thirty-five years when she died. Our relationship began when we were introduced by mutual friends. When Kristine moved to Maine, we began offering weekly groups and workshops based on Gestalt therapy to individuals and couples. As the months progressed, we discovered there was more linking us besides Gestalt therapy. We each had two children, and we realized we were compatible mates highly invested in parenting, and we loved the idea of blending our two little families into one.

I've always kept a journal, and it was a natural thing to do when I felt so overwhelmed by grief. I described on paper what I was feeling. That outlet was helpful when nothing else seemed helpful. My words reflected to me what I was feeling as I wrote them.

This transformation takes both time and awareness, if it comes at all. The process is unpredictable because life keeps unfolding. Who knows what is to come. I feel passionate about this point: a feeling, an emotion, is to be respected, honored, and, it is to be hoped, expressed. The feeling will always prevail, and if it is not acknowledged and expressed, it will manifest physically. Not *maybe* but *will*.

We are humans, so we feel, and whatever the feeling is must be honored. It will out, one way or the other. We can count on it.

Eventually, journaling helped me move through my shock.

Writing every day also gave me the illusion of having some control over my life. I was out of control except for my journaling. Every usual means of measuring my life was gone with Kristine's death and daily absence. Instinctively I knew how to write, and doing so gave me the feeling that I hadn't lost everything, I still had the ability to write. Every so often I'd go back and read what I had written, and what I saw on the pages shocked me. I was learning anew who I was, and I didn't recognize him. Who was this man writing these words? A shock that kept returning to me was that this had happened to me in the first place. How could I still be alive and Kristine be dead? I needed an outlet as this shock transformed into feelings, and writing was natural for me.

I used the journal to mark the passage of time, which was helpful when I felt frozen in despair. I could see that the days were passing, eventually adding up to weeks and months. I was terrified as the first-year anniversary approached because I couldn't stop it from coming. I desperately wanted to be in control. I knew August 3 was coming and I couldn't stop it. I reflected that I'd had no premonition of Kristine's death but it came anyway, unannounced, sudden and shocking. The days marched forward inexorably. Then, suddenly, it came and went. I experienced relief. I also experienced less need to journal every day. I wrote less. Occasionally I skipped a day. I liked the new feeling of not having to write every day, self-imposed as the task was. It were as if I had been released from prison. I had made it through the first year of grieving.

Then I thought that I might have a book. But it was full of my children, and I knew I could not speak for them and what they experienced living with their mother's death. I spent several months editing, trying to concentrate on my own feelings and grieving process.

I discovered not only that was it painful to go back into that first year but also that I didn't need to. The past didn't have much energy. What did have energy was the last chapter of my journal, which was about the gifts that Kristine's death gave me. The gifts were in the present and continued to arrive in my life. I concentrated on describing Kristine's gifts of grief.

Some of us experience our brutal losses without gifts. So be it. All the natural emotions, grief, anger, fear, and love, always and forever come before any potential gifts. Indeed, they are the first harbingers of gifts.

Introduction

If I hadn't found gifts in my grief from losing Kristine, I think I would have ended my life depressed and lonely, possibly early by my own hand. Thankfully and joyously, I have found these gifts.

I wrote many of my feelings that I would normally share with Kristine in my journal. But my journal didn't respond to me in the way that Kristine did. She would look at me with those two different-colored eyes, one blue and one green. That was all she had to do—just look at me. She would nod her head in response to what I was saying. Sometimes she'd offer her own thoughts and feelings— her responses or affirmation and validation.

I didn't know what else to do except write more, so I wrote more.

I learned more about who I was and who I was becoming as a widower. Even now the word "widower" doesn't make any sense to me. There is more to me than that label. I'm in touch with how much less I have in my life, and maybe even how much less of a person I am without Kristine. Yet the gifts show me that I am, at the same time, more.

Nothing I write here ensures that a calamitous loss will produce any gifts. None of my experiences after Kristine died could be another person's. Perhaps gifts never show up. Grief is strong, unexpected, and everlasting. I have come to appreciate these qualities of grief. I can trust my grief. In that way, it is like a companion. I can count on it to return when I need it to, even if I don't know I need it. It is a relief to trust my grief. It means that it's all right to let myself forget about it, because I can trust it to come back when it needs to, or even when I need it to. I can keep it at bay for a while. Eventually I can give in to it only when it comes. I find great relief in that. Grief can't be scheduled. It has its own way, and it has its own way with me. That is what I trust now. It's simply a part of me.

This writing is meant to encourage the expression of grief. This is what happened to me. I offer my encouragement to trust grief and to acknowledge it and find a way to express it. Maybe gifts will appear.

Each chapter begins with the text of a love card that Kristine wrote to me on a special occasion when she felt like it. I am so grateful to have these cards, and I make them an important part of what I am saying—or, that is, Kristine saying what she felt and feels about me.

One

ORANGE SUNSET

Dear Jacob,

How full I feel at this special time of having your birth and life journey– my heart is touched over and over by the love you share with me, my family, your family and all with whom you connect.

Love, Kristine

*T*wo days after our thirty-third wedding anniversary, Kristine and I drove down to my hometown, Marion, Massachusetts, to spend two days with my family for a Watson reunion. Over the previous weekend, we were not sure that Kristine could come, because one of our kids was struggling, but she finally joined me.

My three siblings and I continue to talk every week; we have done so now for about fourteen years. I realize this sibling connection is rare, and we each appreciate it. It began when we realized we needed to be in close touch with each other regarding our parents' increasing needs. We needed to make decisions about their care, medications, and ongoing needs. We were thus able to support them and stay in their house as they aged and eventually died. In doing so, when we had our annual reunions in Marion we were up to date with each other.

My brother lives in Marion, and my sister had flown from California; another sister had driven down from Vermont, and her kids and grandkids were all present. Even my niece and her family came from Chicago. It is a gift that Kristine transported me into the bosom of my family so that I was surrounded by my three loving siblings and all six of their grandchildren.

My first gifts of grief were obscured by the shock. It is a gift, though we had no inkling of it when it was happening, that Kristine, the night we arrived, had her last supper with my family, and they with her. It was not only remarkable to me because it was Kristine's last supper, but also because it was among my family. She was energized, articulate, and engaged, and she talked with many of my family members. She was smiling and genuinely interested in catching up with them. I watched her. I noticed that she was on her own and did not need me. It was a gift that Kristine was this link between the generations. She had known my parents during our many visits and had supported me when my father died, and then two years later when my mother died. Over all the years, she earned her place in the Watson tribe.

My sister again rented the old rustic summer house on the

waterfront in the cove that belongs to distant relatives of ours. It's funky, full of their family stuff, with magnificent views across Meadow Island out to Buzzards Bay. It's near the place where, as a minister, I performed a memorial service some years ago for a dear family elder. There's even a family tree framed on the wall with two of our four names on it.

Kristine and I arrived, had lunch, and immediately, with my sisters and sister-in-law helping, sailed the family Herreshoff 12½ sloop, the *Vireo*, back over to its mooring. With Kristine by my side, we sailed past the old Watson family house, which had been built by my grandfather Lester. It stands now extensively renovated. And then, as we sailed by, there came the precious strip of Watson land where Mum and Dad's house had been until their deaths a few years prior. We children decided to have the house torn down and the waterfront property donated to a land trust. It will be forever wild.

We siblings had agreed years ago on two principles we wanted to govern our decisions going forward. The first was that Mum and Dad's money was theirs, and thus would be used for their care as they lived out their elderhood. The second was that our relationships came first, before any financial concerns. Because we needed to communicate with each other more closely, we began weekly telephone calls to coordinate medicines and helpers for Mum and Dad. We continue those calls today, now on Zoom.

Because our parents had died in their house that was no more, those memories were close by when Kristine and I drove the long driveway to the cove house that morning. It was new to us but old, this house my sister had rented for our summer gatherings. These memories sharpened as we sailed by our old family property and looked at it from the sea, the best vantage point. Without the house now, the land looked empty, serene, and a bit untidy without a human hand to trim the grass. Kristine, in her orange life jacket, took it in, no doubt her many family visits there fresh in her mind.

I could only imagine the many challenges Kristine remembered, having come from the Midwest to join a large Boston WASP family.

In the *Vireo* that fateful afternoon of her final sail, we four looked ashore at the family property. We were quiet as the scene went by our view from the Herreshoff, all of us in our own memories. These were a few deeply precious moments shared without the knowledge of what the next day would bring. It is a gift to know that nothing could have been more fitting than for Kristine to sail by our old family property on her last sail. The abundant treasure trove of her Watson family experiences served as a rich and grateful send-off for her.

On the morning of Kristine's death, my older sister was upstairs. When Kristine went into the bathroom and didn't come out, I noticed the length of time and then the unusual silence. I got worried and knocked on the door. Not getting any response, I opened the door and found her collapsed on the floor. I called her name and shook her but couldn't revive her. Her eyes were closed, and though her body was crumpled, she had a look of peace about her as if she were asleep. This peace burned through my shock and found a place in my heart. I knew Kristine was dead. I was never going to see her blue and brown eyes again.

My sister called the town EMTs. They arrived and tried to restart Kristine's heart. They put her on a gurney and loaded her into the ambulance. But the ambulance sat there in the driveway. I was screaming inside but managed to ask the policeman what was happening, and he said they were preparing her for transport. My sister's daughter showed up from her house a block away and looked into my eyes, not saying anything.

At the hospital, the doctor came into the small white room where I was sitting, pulled his chair up close, and looked right into my eyes. Kristine was dead. I cried on hearing the official words from the official person. Then I was ushered into a much larger room, where Kristine's body was laid out. My sisters and niece appeared on the other side of the gurney, these three strong family women standing together. They sang "Amazing Grace," then left me with Kristine's body, alone. Her eyes were closed. She looked peaceful, asleep. I imagined that I saw her eyes open. It wasn't just her eyes; it was the crinkles around them as well. Her eyes were two different colors; her left was blue and her right was brown. Now they were closed, and my mind said that they were closed forever. I wanted to reach over and pry them open to see them again, just to see the fire and energy sparkle in them. But I couldn't argue with the peace that I saw right now. It was the same peace that I had seen when I went into our bathroom that morning. Peace now. Peace forever.

I was to see her closed eyes one more time in my life, at the funeral home viewing in Portland. Again, in that simple room that her presence filled, I felt peace.

Now I sat there in my chair, in shock, staring at Kristine. I was sitting with Kristine, yet I could not feel her. I held her hand and touched her face, and I kissed her. Nothing. Just peace. No response. I waited. I sat there on and on. I felt lonely—the first twinges of loneliness. There was nothing I could do except sit there in the chair. I prayed. I meditated. I sat there. The room felt cold. Finally, I got up, but I didn't want to leave Kristine. I sat down again and waited, but nothing changed. Just peace. It was a hint of a gift that showed me Kristine was now in another form.

Eventually I stood up. I couldn't find a way out of the room. I did not want to go back and sit in the chair. I saw a doorway, went out into the hallway, and found my way down to a room where my sisters were waiting for me. I realized I didn't want to be in the hospital building, so I stumbled outside, where I found a small garden with a bench. I sat there trembling, knowing I had to make phone calls to my children that would change their lives. When picking up my phone, I didn't feel Kristine with me at all. I don't think I've ever felt so alone. I made the calls one by one. I experienced my children responding in their own unique ways, deep in the shock of this sudden tragic news. They gasped. I learned later that one collapsed and fell to the ground. They worried about me.

I was dimly aware of my two sisters watching me from a respectful distance at the edge of the garden. When I finished and got up from the bench, I walked out into the street, and my sisters had to guide me to our car.

Back at the house, I sat alone outside on the swinging couch. A brown hummingbird came from my right side, hovered back and forth, then darted in front of me. It was Kristine, come to check on me to see if I was all right. She was reassured, gave a tiny smile, and flew away, back off to the right.

After a subdued supper, I went outdoors and sat on the back steps. My sister pointed out a beautiful orange sunset over the upper end of the cove. I hadn't seen it. The whole sky reflected spectacularly on the calm, shallow water at the head of the cove. The color was brilliant, bright and alive, more to herald a beginning than an ending of a day or a life.

I sat on the steps and contemplated. Kristine was alive when this day began; she was not alive when it ended. The day was now ending while we watched the sun set slowly yet inexorably.

We stayed on the steps for a long time, talking and making a mental list of things to remember to do the following day. I didn't write anything down on a piece of paper. This was the beginning of not making lists. I knew that my old reliance on writing things down on a piece of paper was no longer relevant. This was new territory. I knew in my bones that if something was important to me, I would remember it.

My sister's gangly teenage grandson came and sat on the grass near us for a while, his quiet presence both shocking and comforting.

It was a gift to me that, sitting there, I could remember the previous spring, when Kristine and I had talked again about our wishes after we died. We had settled on one funeral home to call to make arrangements. It was a small local company right in our neighborhood.

It was a gift to me that I knew without thinking what I wanted to use to cover Kristine's sacred body at the viewing: the scarf her granddaughter had given her. And for a blanket, I would use the hospice quilt from her upstairs yoga room. It has individual squares created by the volunteers Kristine trained, as well as staff members. It was put together by a hospice nurse for Kristine's hospice farewell party. It was a fitting symbol of Kristine's dedication to making good matches between a hospice volunteer she had trained and the family needing services. Because Kristine was modest, the quilt served as an enduring symbol of the appreciation and respect of hospice staff, volunteers, and family for Kristine's sensitive skills.

Even in the midst of all the despair I felt from losing my partner, I felt deeply connected to my hometown. My brother lives there, as do four or five cousins. The family property, a slice of which we siblings gave to a land trust, is now forever wild. It is overgrown and lies peacefully on the town harbor shore. I return every summer for a family reunion, and if I'm lucky I see over the calm evening harbor water some variation of Kristine's bright orange sunset.

Two

MONARCH BUTTERFLIES

Dear Jacob,

Walking with you through these years has brought me laughter, tears, joy and immense love! May we keep upright, healthy and enjoying nature together!

Love, Kristine

After a sleepless night, around noon my sister and I left for Maine, she driving my car. It was strange to be sitting in the passenger seat, but I was glad to let her drive. I felt confused because I was leaving Kristine but going home to the house we shared. In fact, I didn't really know where Kristine was. Her body was somewhere between Marion and Portland. We had driven down to Marion together, and now I was going home without her. Where was Kristine?

My rational mind, in shock, remembered that I had given permission for the donation of Kristine's organs so she would be giving gifts to others, as she always had. That meant her body was being transported to the funeral home a few blocks from our house. Even in shock, I could see this as a gift. As if by magic, she would be in Portland when I got home. This question of where Kristine was, was to haunt me for months. I had to come up with my own answers.

Gradually, way too slowly for me, I realized that her spirit was still with me. But because I'm human, I missed her physical presence beside me in the car. On the long drive, I began to understand that I was, and would be for years, living out two roles: that of a griever and of the father of my four grieving children. All of my children, to my relief, came to accept me as their grieving father. I was relieved because I could be myself and didn't have to pretend otherwise.

When I stepped onto the deck at home in Portland, I was glad to be in familiar surroundings, but they didn't feel familiar. To the right, Kristine's garden, with its red and yellow flowers, welcomed me. But she wasn't beside me; nor was she in the garden in her orange shirt. A glaze was covering everything; I later understood this to be the glaze of grief. Still, being home was comforting.

I had many tasks to do, and while they were horrendous, only I could do them, and I knew that. I remembered my decision not to write anything down in lists, and I was glad not to see anything in black and white on a piece of paper. Leaving time—days—between calls, I let my relatives and friends know that Kristine had died. Every time I called, I had to listen anew to their shock and dismay. I walked over to my three nearest neighbors and told them. They gave me hugs, which I appreciated. But I didn't stay long.

I didn't know what to do with Kristine's bags and clothes from our trip to Marion, so I put them by her dresser in our bedroom. Every time I turned a corner or went into a different room in our house, I expected Kristine to be there to help with these tasks, but she wasn't.

What I had to do felt mysterious and overwhelming, but I had my four children to do it with me. Well, not with me exactly, because much of our grief was personal, and it came up every time we did one of these tasks. At least I know I wasn't alone. I asked them, and they did the tasks on their own and reported back to me.

It seemed as if most of the tasks were for me to do. I talked with a funeral service, the one Kristine and I had chosen here in our neighborhood. How many death certificates did I want? None. But I had to decide on a number. Then, a week later, I had to drive down to the funeral home to pick them up, chastely sealed in a manila envelope, glued shut. Then I had to open them, and the official blue certificate repulsed me. I was caught between "Kristine's death must be," and "It can't be."

I called our life insurance company to look up numbers in a manila folder. I called the City of Portland and places like the property and automobile insurance company. I opened her mail, but it felt like an invasion of privacy. But who else was going to do it?

It was a gift to have Kristine's body transported without charge from Marion because I was able to arrange to donate some of her organs.

A day later, a small group of family gathered at the funeral chapel nearby. I included our dear friend who was to be the facilitator for Kristine's memorial service. We were still in shock and preparing for more when we saw Kristine's body. We were ushered down the pews of a chapel and into a drab room. There was Kristine's body. We had to bring our own chairs in to sit down. But we didn't sit down. Her body, with the scarf and hospice quilt, lay so still. Her presence filled the room in a way that I didn't understand. It was no longer a drab room. Kristine lived there. She was at peace, as we could see. We each had time with her, then it was time to go. I will always remember that room as shimmering with Kristine's light.

Soon we thought of having a memorial service for Kristine at Portland Head Light, on the ocean, which was a place she loved. We had brought her family there when they visited from Michigan. It was a place that we knew as a family, and where Kristine and I had helped organize Hospice fundraising events. One day, having steeled myself, I drove out to Portland Head Light alone. Driving over the familiar roads out to the sea felt like a sacred pilgrimage for me. I was very conscious of being alone. I drove into the parking lot beneath the picnic area. The sun was so bright I couldn't see the numbers on the machine to pay for my parking space, or maybe it was my tears. I just left the car there without paying and walked up the hill. No one was around, so I took my time. I couldn't imagine coming back in two weeks for Kristine's service when there would be other people. The place looked so empty now, with the large picnic tables set out in angular rows. I worried that nobody would attend. Wouldn't people be uncomfortable perched on the picnic table seats? I looked down from the picnic area and saw tourists walking around together and strolling down to the iconic red-roofed lighthouse perched precariously on the rocky cliff. I wanted to be out on the water on a sailboat heading out to sea, not trapped by the land.

Since the picnic place felt appropriate to me, I didn't have anything to do except walk around and try to imagine people showing up. But my imagination faltered. I left the tables and walked out onto the green grass of the field nearby. Suddenly a cloud of monarch butterflies, black and orange, swarmed in front of me and proceeded to accompanying me as I walked. I started to cry. I could feel Kristine's spirit with me, and I wasn't alone. I felt strength combine with my fragility. I knew those qualities so well in Kristine. She was so fragile that she had died. She was so strong that she was still with me. That was all I needed. I didn't have to do anything except keep walking and keep my eyes on the butterflies just ahead of me. I recalled that Kristine and I had walked these same steps many times before, getting ready for a hospice event. I was not even lonely anymore.

I didn't know what else to do except keep our reservation for the camp that we—really Kristine—had rented months prior. This would be the third summer we rented this place, about forty-five minutes away. It gave us a place to be together and things to do for ourselves amid this tragedy. The wide lake beckoned as it had for many years to generations of families. We realized it might be a soothing place for us to be together. There was nothing to do except cook our meals and hang out on the lake together amid these strange, sad circumstances. We all missed Kristine, the central figure of our family, yet we were with each other in our grief.

In the morning, I was grateful that my granddaughter came over and helped me get cereal for breakfast on the porch. We washed blueberries, poured the milk and the cereal into bowls, and took them out to the porch. I put my hearing aids in, which helped a lot. I recognized that this was an important time that would allow her and our family to see and feel how we might navigate through this time without Kristine. Sharing breakfast together was a good beginning.

At night we began to talk about the service for Kristine, and we focused first on who would be the facilitator. I talked with Kristine's longtime friend who was also a hospice chaplain and Buddhist priest. I brought up my concern that he was also grieving Kristine's death. After discussing this, he said he could manage his grief adequately to do the service.

It is a gift to me that Kristine's one true cherished friend agreed to be her memorial service facilitator. I remembered well how they would meet every couple of months for three hours at a time, at either his place, a Zen monastery nearby, or in Kristine's office. They had the same birthday, though in different years, and shared a rare and deep trust that defined their friendship. They exchanged intimate secrets of their lives with each other. He was the perfect person to lead her memorial gathering even as he was grieving her loss. My family and I trusted his chaplain experience and, even more, his love of Kristine.

I had the feeling that he didn't want anybody else to do this service, which was true for me too. We both knew he was the right person to do it. He would give the proceedings an authenticity we all cherished. I believed that Kristine would have wanted him to do it. He agreed to come out to camp to meet with all of us that week. I was relieved. We all were.

One morning, my meditative gaze out on to the calm lake was joined by a little sparrow that flew up onto the porch railing. I could see it from the couch, bobbing about, hopping closer and closer. It took a good, long look at me and, satisfied, hopped once more and flew away to rejoin her companions. To me, this was Kristine checking on me.

It was wonderful to see my family embrace and thank Kristine's friend for coming out to camp to help us plan the service. They could feel that we were in good hands.

To prepare for this service, I measured Kristine's hospice quilt so we could hang it, and I gathered photographs to share. I cried while driving out to check the picnic site for the service one last time, and I cried lots more while driving back. I felt quite alone. My children and their partners helped with the details of Kristine's service. That morning, reassured by the warm weather, we set up the chairs facing the ocean that we could see through the trees. I didn't know how I' was doing or what I needed. I needed Kristine. I began to say what I had repeated many times: "I could get through this grief if Kristine were here with me. It is a difficult gift to accept that I must do this on my own, but it is nevertheless a gift. I can now harvest my own resources." I said to my kids at camp that I wanted Kristine to help me find them, to get me through this. And she did so, though from a great distance.

It is a gift that our memorial ceremony at Fort Williams Park to honor Kristine was an extraordinary demonstration that she had many friends—friends who were missing her. If only she had been there, the misunderstanding that she did not have friends would have been dispelled for her. In fact, she was loved by many people: our big family, of course, and many others in the Portland community.

After the facilitator's heartfelt introduction, he nodded to me. I stood up and took a few steps to the front of the gathering. Then I turned around. Suddenly, with a force that disarmed me, I saw with my own eyes what Kristine never knew: that she had many friends. Here they were. They sat on the picnic benches, quietly expectant. The first words out of my mouth were "Kristine was a truth-teller. This is awful. This is a disaster in my life and in the life of my family. Grief is *brutal*." I described the morning Kristine died and explained my feeling brutalized by this sudden loss of my dear companion. I said I was deeply grateful to look out and see that many people came to honor Kristine. I couldn't say any more.

Later I remembered I had wanted to share that Kristine and I loved a song by Kate Wolf. We chose the words "gentle warrior" to inscribe in her wedding ring, and the words "spirit healer" for mine. To all who knew and loved her, Kristine was indeed a gentle warrior. Because the words described not only us but also our relationship, I had the lyrics printed in the program.

Even though I forgot to say this out loud, Kristine's friends did take the song lyrics in the program with them when they left. They just didn't know that those two phrases were inscribed in our wedding rings.

Then my eldest daughter spoke, spontaneously, with her tears flowing, about Kristine's quiet strength. She described her own dedication to keeping our family together without Kristine here. She promised that we would stay together as a family. She felt lucky that Kristine and I had wonderful years together. She finished by saying, "I love you all."

My sister spoke, with tears, about missing Kristine and read the sweet letter from our other sister in California. She described how vibrant Kristine was at the large family meal the night before she died.

Then the facilitator invited those gathered to share their feelings about Kristine. Many did. Kristine's friends shared the ways she had been part of their lives and contributed to their healing. The theme was gratitude, mixed with sadness that Kristine's life was over. The words bathed us in solace, each appreciation a personal gift. We were held by the sea, the cawing of the black crows, and the salty wind moving noisily through the big, old trees. How could they be anything but gifts to us all?

After people shared, my daughter and the mother of my only grandchild stood up and walked to the front. When she turned around to speak, she was silent. She looked slowly around at everyone gathered there. They looked at her. It was courageous of her, because as she looked at them, they were looking at her in her grief. Her face showed it. She read a poem from Kristine's sister in Michigan. Then the service was over. I stayed in my chair, not trusting myself to stand up, and some people came over to talk with me. I appreciated that a lot. I could see the grief on their faces. Then there was nobody in front of me. I turned and watched as Kristine's friends walked away. I felt comfort that most of them were holding the program that my daughter-in-law had made for the service. I felt that a little piece of Kristine was going home with them. And I remembered the Buddhist prayer that the facilitator had said out loud as part of the service, which was printed next to the purple lupines. It read,

> With every breath I take today,
> I vow to be awake;
> and every step I take, I vow to
> take with a grateful heart –
> So I may see with eyes of love,
> into the hearts of all I meet,
> To ease their burden when I can and
> touch them with a smile of peace.

After people drifted away, we took down the hospice quilt, photographs, and flowers. I was exhausted and glad to have a family member drive me home. I felt relieved to be back in the house and just wanted to be alone, because that's how I was—alone. Well-meaning family members hung around for a while—reluctant to leave me by myself, I imagine. But the truth is that I was now by myself. I was glad when everybody left. The sudden solitude felt like a gift.

I was now alone but couldn't change my history with Kristine. The furniture store emailed that the couch Kristine and I had ordered six months prior had arrived and was ready to be delivered. I felt so sad Kristine was not here to receive it with me. It's for the Connecticut family when they come to visit. Kristine will never hear how pleased they are to have a comfortable bed in the house.

We had shopped for the couch together, driving out to the mall and visiting three furniture stores. Then we walked into one in Portland, and the sales clerk recognized us from our hospice work. We were well taken care of and felt again our place in the community. Here it was, months later, when everything had changed. The couch wouldn't be arriving unless Kristine and I had ordered it together. It was proof that she had been here.

One of Kristine's daughters, responding to how I looked at the moment, gave me a hug. While we were close, she whispered to me, "We're going to get through this." With unsparing instinct, she chose the precise moment when I wasn't sure we were going to get through this at all. Her remarkable resilience buoyed me when I most needed it.

On my morning walk, when I approached my house on Glenwood Avenue, a mourning dove joined me, walking in the gutters of several houses and cooing softly to me before it flew off. I felt Kristine's presence again in nature.

The park is still there by the ocean, cradling the iconic lighthouse built at the behest of George Washington. I visit occasionally, sometimes on my own, sometimes with family members. We gaze up at the now sacred picnic grounds where we had our memorial service for Kristine. The butterflies still visit in the fall. Maybe I will see them; maybe I won't. They, like this human life, are fragile. The many miles they travel are part of their history, just as Kristine is part of my history. I do not wish anything to be different, and that is a relief, a further gift.

Three

ENGLISH TEAPOT

Jacob,

You captured my heart many years ago and I am glad for that! Thank you for the years of love– may we deepen into our elderly years with grace!

Love you, Kristine

ristine was missing everywhere I looked inside the house. The bed upstairs was now empty instead of two loving bodies; now it contained only one body—mine. I didn't know when to change the sheets. *Who is going to help me fold the clean sheets after I wash them? Especially the bottom fitted sheet. When I need heat in the cold winter, do I turn on her side of the electric blanket or not?* What if I drifted over to Kristine's side in the middle of the night, looking for her? I might be repelled by the chill and return to my side, chastened but probably not really awake, and certainly not warmed.

I had to buy and cook one-person portions and eat them by myself. I didn't like it at first because it was a reminder of what was missing. With time and practice, I got good at shopping for myself. I learned my way around one particular grocery store so I knew where things were. I developed a certain independence that I liked. Unconsciously at first, I followed my mother's prescription from the days of my childhood to finish my food because there are hungry people in the world. I needed to eat with gratitude for what I had. This rediscovery forced me to finish what I put on my plate.

Kristine's absence at the table was severe. I sat by myself. I ate by myself. I find there's such a thin line between "ate" and "ache." This gift came only with time, as I came to appreciate that I could shop and cook for myself. indeed this gift expanded over time as I learned that I could take complete care of myself.

I discovered Kristine's computer cord attached to her machine that she would never use again. I realized I could switch cords to replace mine, which was torn. Was it okay to do? I brought her cord downstairs and plugged my computer into it. The current flowed through Christine's cord and into my machine. Kristine would have approved.

I like a clean house, and I was determined to show myself I could take care of it, so I dusted, and I even laughed at myself because of the conversations I had with Kristine. She would always dust, and I would never dust; I didn't even know how to do it right. I vacuumed downstairs because it reminded me of Kristine and because she would like me to have a clean house.

I noticed the dusted furniture and the clean rug most when I was sitting in front of the TV.

The best show I found about grief is *After Life*, a British series about a newspaper reporter who loses his wife. I sat in the living room and watched it and let my tears come. Nothing else I tried to watch made any sense or had any meaning. I rebelled against watching TV at all. It was too lonely and too time-consuming, and it filled my head with meaningless trivia. I didn't care what was happening in the world. I especially didn't want to watch any news programs. So I didn't, and it was a relief. I didn't want to sit in the living room at all, clean or not.

It is a gift to let go of the personal routine and cultural imperative of watching TV football every Sunday. Since Kristine died, I have been free of that commercial violence. Even March Madness, the NCAA college basketball tournament that usually featured our daughter's college team, fell by the wayside. Suddenly the March weekends were free.

It is a gift that I am not attached to any of Kristine's things, such as her clothes or books. I was attached to her, not what she wore or read. I encouraged her daughters to go through her clothes and make decisions: save or take to Goodwill. I give them plenty of time—many months. I have a good friend who takes anything I give him. He donates it to immigrants who arrive here in Portland with no household items or clothes. I feel a freedom, the ease of nonattachment, and I loved knowing that Kristine would have approved.

When I go into Kristine's upstairs room, which we called her yoga room, I see her hospice quilt hanging on the wall to the left. Sometimes I take the time to read the brief gratitudes sewn by the senior hospice nurse into a quilt for Kristine's hospice retirement party.

In the morning, I hear my daughter and her husband outside, sitting in in the two white rocking chairs—a delightful way for me to wake up. I am full of gratitude. But they used to be our kids, and now they are my kids. They hold hands a lot at mealtimes. I love seeing the gesture, and sadness comes because I do not have Kristine to hold hands with.

Kristine is free from her anxiety, depression, and worry, not to mention all the physical aches and pains. Kristine and I had made specific plans to drive out to Michigan for her niece's wedding. She had made reservations at hotels along the way, and on the way home we had planned to stop at the Rock and Roll Hall of Fame and Niagara Falls. I asked my son to cancel the reservations Kristine had made. I was relieved that he soon had all arrangements cancelled and our deposits returned.

When I finally went upstairs and got into bed late at night, I tried to console myself by listening to old hippie music: Crosby, Stills, Nash and Young; Jackson Browne (especially his song "The Pretender"); Bruce Springsteen's "You're Missing"; and, of course, Dylan and his song "Forever Young." Sometimes I would put on classical music during the day. As I walked through the empty house, I reflected that this music had been played for generations, and that was soothing to me. I then felt less alone.

Kristine and I created, both consciously and unconsciously, a whole set of schedules and routines to live together in our house. When Kristine died, I discovered a fierce need to keep these the same as much as possible. It became an obsession, really. It was my feeble attempt to pretend that my life had not changed dramatically. This had to do with both the household and my schedule every day. It was the way I thought I was holding myself together. Continuing my spiritual practices did help me a lot. I include all my daily routines in these because they were, for me, spiritual practices. They started early in the morning, as I was waking up alone. I couldn't change that. But I could change how I woke up. I set my iPhone to wake me up earlier than usual, at six thirty. To wake me up, I programmed a soft melody sung by an Irish friend I met when we staffed Elisabeth Kübler-Ross workshops.

I came downstairs to Kristine's empty seat in the kitchen facing the gas heat stove. I sat at the small, round wooden table that looks nautical. Kristine had bought the table in Freeport on sale, knowing I would appreciate its nautical design. I still do.

I had the upstairs bathroom sink replaced because the old sink bowl was beginning to deteriorate and it was hard to clean properly. I sat in my office downstairs, and the plumber's helper came downstairs and into my room holding in front of her the backsplash to the old sink. She reached me and turned it over, and there was Kristine's name written in black magic marker on the back: "Kristine Watson." A clerk at the plumbers' supply store wrote it so that we would get the correct sink. There it was, and there she was, still in my house, my life. She will always be in my heart no matter where I go. Nothing can change the fact that she so often shows up unexpectedly like this. I felt feelings of sadness and loss, as well as a powerful kind of invincibility. I could absolutely count on the fact that Kristine was going to show up. And I knew that If I could survive this, I could survive anything. I don't want these reminders, but they show up on a regular basis.

Upstairs around the corner from our bedroom is the bathroom that Kristine and I had renovated over a decade before. Up high behind the door, Kristine created two ornamental shelves with white filigree. She placed there a colorful curving peacock feather rising out of artwork by a former counseling client. A small white wooden box held a blue-and-white rowboat. It was clearly not something I would have created but came from Kristine's artistic side. Now every time I walk in the bathroom my head swivels to the left and I take in her creation.

Right across the hall is Kristine's yoga room with the blue dresser where she kept her electric English teapot. I bought it for her to make her morning Earl Grey tea. After she died, it sat unused on her dresser opposite her desk. A year went by, and there was buzz about gas stoves emitting toxic fumes, which Kristine would have heeded. I brought her teapot down to the kitchen and put it on the counter beside the refrigerator. I use it to heat my morning green tea. Every time I use it, I thank Kristine for her gift.

After almost a year, when a neighbor who had been a counseling client of Kristine's came over for tea, she was amazed that she had died. She thought Kristine might be here. I don't know who was more shocked—she or me. Because she had been a client of Kristine's, she knew her well, but she had not seen her obituary. All of our subsequent conversation, normal as it seemed, was haunted by her responses to hearing of Kristine's death and not seeing her anywhere in the house in physical form. The same was true for me. I was talking with someone who knew us both but who had just found out about Kristine's death.

Kristine was just short of a hoarder, with the best of intentions: to provide for her family. We had a lot of stuff, and it was Kristine's way of making sure that all of us had everything we needed. Kristine left me with a household full of supplies, upstairs and down, as well as the basement and the garage. Some was food in the kitchen cupboards. All the closets were full, and the drawers and living room and bedroom shelves as well. I realized that we hadn't gotten rid of much when the kids moved out years ago. They didn't take much with them. I discovered towels everywhere: hand towels, bath towels, beach towels, and ragged-edged towels that we used for cleaning. I found enough birthday and Christmas wrapping paper, especially tissue paper, for years to come. As with the other gifts Kristine left me, every time I use them, I say a quiet thank-you to her. When rapping new Christmas presents, now from just me, I remember how carefully Kristine wrapped her gifts, especially those for our children. I do it in my own way, not as neat, but the paper and ribbon come from Kristine. I have lots of time to rub my hands on her paper, because it takes me four or five tries to tie the ribbon with my clumsy fingers.

She left me the house plants in the living room and dining room. I know enough to water them occasionally, but that is all. They sit there growing green. One died, and I felt guilty.

Because (unlike that house plant) they're still with me, I have new appreciation for the tangible gifts that Kristine gave me: the big Delta table saw for my shop down in the cellar, the custom-made wooden cabinet for my incense and candles for meditation, the big Weber grill on the deck. She saw my need for these, and way before I thought we could afford them, she bought them and gave them to me.

All this reminds me that Kristine is not here in the human realm. She is missing. But I still feel her. She must be in the spiritual realm. How to connect? She's changed, not me. But maybe I can change, to be closer to her. It is now true for me that everything leads to the spiritual realm.

For example, I realize that the Huck Finn etching I received in the mail from the Portland Museum of Art depicts me grieving. I hung it on my office wall, and Huck Finn, slumped over and exhausted on the raft, watches me out of the corner of his eye as I meditate many mornings.

For years the radiator in the front hall needed repainting. Kristine wasn't here to remind me. I walked by it every time I came downstairs, and anybody who came in the house through the front door saw it, paint peeling. I thought about it for months, imagining how Kristine would remind me or do it herself. I finally bought the paint, got the sandpaper and paint scraper up from the cellar, and found a paintbrush. They sat by the radiator for two weeks. Finally came the day when I painted it, with Kristine's spirit chuckling at my shoulder, urging me on. It took me a whole day because there were lots of surfaces to cover. Then it was done. I felt Kristine's approval of my taking care of the house.

At first I didn't dare touch any of Kristine's clothes. I didn't mind having them around, because I still hoped she would appear any minute and get into them. But all too slowly, that changed. After months, I realized I had never opened her dresser drawers. But I knew the clothes were in there, lurking. I had avoided opening the drawers because I knew her clothes were in there, looking at me, waiting for me to do something. I told her daughters that I wanted to clean out the dresser. I'd stopped saying "our bedroom" because it wasn't ours anymore. That language felt better.

Months went by. Then one afternoon I was having a glass of wine with an old friend whose wife had died about two months earlier. He described how he was getting rid of her clothes and making the bedroom and the whole house his. He had put some of his own clothes in his wife's dresser. A lightbulb went off; I was shocked. I had never thought to use Kristine's dresser myself, not to mention space in the closets in other rooms. I was stunned by my lack of perception. I didn't know why I hadn't thought of moving my own clothes into Kristine's spaces. But I hadn't. Then I moved some of my clothes into her dresser. The move was only about eighteen inches. I did it quickly, perhaps worried that somebody would accuse me of something. Right away I felt the expansion of myself into formerly empty spaces. The bedroom felt more whole with me taking up more space. It was a positive feeling.

I asked my children to go through her other clothes and shoes in the closets. I was balancing my need, which I felt but couldn't explain, with their need. The day came when I was ready to empty out the closets. When I finally made this decision, I wanted to do it quickly. I opened the two closets, and there they were—Kristine's clothes, still hanging there peacefully, as if they were waiting for me. All the items were on hangers, and I didn't know whether to take the hangers. I decided to take all the clothes off the hangers. I wrapped my arms around them. My arms felt wrapped around Kristine. I embraced her. I took them downstairs and out to the trunk of my car. It took me three trips. I drove out to the Goodwill donation center, which we'd used in the past when together we went on cleaning-out binges. I drove into the parking lot and around to the drop-off center and saw a yellow chain around it with a sign that said it was closed. I pulled over in the parking lot and located another donation center. But it was time to go meet a friend at a coffee shop.

I was early, so I ordered my small mocha and sat on a couch, waiting. The couch was near the pickup counter, where people's drinks were being called out. I was sitting in the morning sun, still in a daze because Kristine 's clothes were in my car. Then, as loud and clear as a bell, the barista called out "Kristine." I jolted awake. I fought back an urge to look around, then I did look around. The sound of her name echoed in the busy coffee shop. I kept breathing. Soon my friend came, and I told him what had happened. He agreed to take Kristine's clothes when we finished our coffees and take them over to donate to the immigrants and refugees arriving in Portland. For me it was much better than dumping them into an anonymous Goodwill bin. Given the circumstances, it was the best way I could have said good-bye to Kristine's clothes—a gift.

I can now get rid of the brown pillowcases that I never liked anyway. This is one example of the freedom Kristine has given me.

It is a gift that she left me with a well-stocked, functioning house. Everything works, inside and out; all the appliances are working. Kristine knew when to do the annual maintenance chores, such as cleaning out the gutter over the deck, getting the chimney cleaned, and revitalizing the gardens—front, back and both sides. She loved her time messing about in our gardens.

Kristine lives on in the photographs and books in the house, both upstairs and down. I haven't changed anything of these. I love seeing them. I often forget why I'm in that area because I get lost in the memories the photographs bring back. Most of them are of us, but some predate our meeting each other and go back to our early histories. I don't begrudge being lost in them, because they are a part of my life, and it's good to be reminded. They are as much a part of this house as the English teapot, only more so because they go further back in time. And because they go further back, they also go forward in time. Eventually our children will take them into their own homes, and they will be a legacy of Kristine's and my relationship.

Four

GREEN LEAF HARBORS

Dear Jacob,

The moments are sweet, the present feels warm and loving, the future holds the gift of it all.

I love you, Kristine

ristine was everywhere outside the house too, on our little piece of property in the city that we loved. Her spirit lives in our little front garden and in the four square granite posts we had installed in the sidewalk out front. She loved digging in the dirt. A common joke between us was how she often forgot to wear her garden gloves, causing her hands to become black from the soil.

Once, a friend who is a professional gardener came over. He stood at the top of our back garden with Kristine and me and looked carefully at our lawn and back garden beneath our neighbor's fence. He waved his hand and made a powerful suggestion. He said we could change the straight line between the garden and the lawn into a curved boundary. It was brilliant and changed the way the yard felt. Kristine and I together made the change. I dug into the sod with a spade, and Kristine brought more dirt down from the garden to make a slightly curving separation. The arc we created shifted the way the whole yard looked, softening both the grass lawn and the flowers. In a magical way, this deepened their relationship to each other. Kristine loved to dig in the old city dirt, adding compost to make it richer, especially in the back gardens.

I feel her soul in the earth and the colorful flowers that emerged and later allowed her spirit to shine forth. Each little precious and brave flower, and there are many, is a gift from Kristine. When they finally fade as summer comes to an end, I miss these reminders of Kristine but rejoice in joining the cycle of the seasons. I even have come to welcome the colder temperatures that Kristine loved.

Inspired by my brother's peaceful pond that I visit every winter in Florida, I bought a little bamboo water fountain. I set it up near our back garden. I love its clear, meditative gurgling. I remember reading Alan Watts's words, "You hear the sound of water, and that's quite as important as anything I've got to say." I sit surrounded by the beauty of Kristine's colorful flowers and the soft sound of the water fountain. They provide the perfect background for my meditation time.

Often I sit there in peaceful silence way beyond the bell that signifies the end of my usual meditation time. I am peaceful out on the deck, listening to the bright chorus of morning birds singing in the background. I watch a little butterfly, so fragile its whole being, as wings of a special yellow-white, almost translucent, arise from Kristine's garden. It wobbles and weaves its way among the green plant leaves—a message to me from Kristine that all is well.

I often reflect that while I was meditating, I might have been surrounded by such colorful butterflies, all of them giving me that same message. Indeed, the part of Kristine that is still here delights in the blue, red, and yellow flowers coming up in the gardens around the house. This was her meditation time as she tended them.

Years ago, when it came time to buy a new car, we did the research together. Kristine was adamant that she wanted a special blue color. It was the particular dark blue of a flower she planted in the front garden. Now every time I see the car in the garage, or in parking lots, I thank Kristine for choosing a beautiful dark blue. The color is a statement that you can have what you want, you can take the extra time to choose the exact color you want in your life, either in your garden or in your garage. By simple extension, you can have anything that you want in your life, which was an ideal that Kristine taught to her clients and struggled to live in her life. Whether it was curtains, flowers, clothes, or artwork, Kristine had a sense of color that she shared with all of us and that is still with me, with that deeper message.

Sitting on the deck, I imagine that the blue sky over our house in Portland is an ocean. In the foreground overhead are the copious green leaves of our neighbor's trees. I appreciate them greatly because we don't have any trees on our property. As I look up, they create a green coastline of harbors, as if I were looking at a chart of coastal Maine that I know well. I find in the sky configurations of leaves that create shelter from the winds and waves out at sea. I know I am seeking shelter from the storm of losing Kristine. I find safe harbors overhead in the trees. I imagine a little sailboat, like the one I had when I was younger, the little Bristol 27 sloop, making its steady way into the calm harbors overhead.

I came to realize that shelter was all around me. I discovered that there were safe harbors everywhere that protected me from the storms of the open ocean. I learned over the months I sat out on the deck, even in the winter, that I have shelter everywhere, if I can only see it. I realized that every tree within my vision has safe harbors outlined in its leaves. Each of my two neighbors on either side had trees with safe harbors. Even the faraway trees in the next block, the ones whose trunks disappeared down into neighborhood houses, fences and shrubs, had safe harbors. These were less distinct but were present for me nonetheless.

For a while I thought I was simply a sailor eager to find a protected harbor or an idle task to do while I sat in the chair on the deck. But no, I was longing for a safe harbor to protect me from the storms of grief in the open ocean of my life. The little inlets, encircled by the green leafy and protective shorelines, and the black bare branches that I imagined as breakwaters gave me quiet, secure anchorages in which I could rest. I received additional comfort knowing that every green leaf and black branch came up from the earth underneath me.

One evening as I sat out on the deck, I watched a hummingbird approach the feeder in the back garden. This was unusual; no hummingbird had visited the feeder until then, as I sat there. The small brown-and-red hummingbird came from the driveway side, flew close to the feeder, and circled it twice. It flew away to the left without drinking from the feeder. I remembered sitting in the garden outside the house my sister had rented in Marion on the August day Kristine died. A brown hummingbird also had come from my right side, flown in front of me, fluttered quietly for a few seconds, and flown off. Again I was guessing that this was Kristine in spirit forevermore.

It is a gift to me from Kristine that she loved the fall season and its dropping temperatures. I didn't like it at first, because I got cold. I was okay in January once winter had set in, but not in October and November. Kristine loved that time of year. She embraced the coming of the frost and the changing of the seasons. Now I do too, because it reminds me of her. I bundle up during the day and at night to make sure I'm warm. I even bought myself a cozy red fleece throw from L.L. Bean. Kristine would want me to be warm.

Many gifts from the natural world remind me of Kristine: the hummingbirds, that glorious sunset over the cove the night of the day she died, the little sparrow at camp, and the little feather I found at home. Chippy the chipmunk comes for visits and peers cautiously up over the edge of the deck. I see the glorious and immense blue sky, which holds Kristine's essence. The very atmosphere, the air itself of our home at 41 Glenwood Avenue in Portland, holds her. This place, inside and out, gave her a home when she was alive and gives her a home now. The very air is thick with her in a most loving way. It holds me and nurtures me. It's why I laughed when a well-meaning friend asked me whether I was going to move out of the house. I'll probably stay here as long as I live.

All the conversations that Kristine and I had with each other about staying here as we aged began with "we." Now I am by myself, so I don't know. I feel as if I don't know anything. But I do know I love this house. This is my home, and I plan to stay here as long as I can. I think Kristine would want this for me. Indeed, she would consider me staying here as a gift she gave me. The countless little and big tasks she did were all to create a home for us, and now I know she would want me to enjoy all of that.

All the colorful plants and flowers, inside and out, continue to grow. After a long Maine winter of hiding, the green grass, the flowers, and especially the pink Chime rose bush by the deck blossom in the spring and sprout forth new growth. Whether I'm having a day consumed by grief or any other of the natural emotions, such as anger, fear, and love, the sprouts emerge. I sit in my meditative place, soothed by the gurgling water, and drink in the growth around me, and the green harbors overhead. I can smell the flowers as they gain strength and color and come into their own. I don't have to do anything except just enjoy them, and I do. Memories of Kristine in our gardens abound. They are interwoven with all the leaves and the new petals I see. It is her creative spirit that lives on.

Five

MEMORIAL STAR

Dear Jacob,

Traveling through these years has reminded me each day to put my best self forward. Thank you! I love you, Kristine

*I*t is a gift that I now realize our goal of creating a blended family worked well when the children were young. It gave the four of them a good beginning to their lives. Then it changed with the passage of time and now suddenly with Kristine's death. The gift is to understand that my children know that I love them, and I know that they love me. They have survived being blended and now are grown up. Like most parents, I experience a gap between how I would like our children to relate to each other and the reality of the situation. When Kristine died, all four of our children showed up for me when I most needed them. Each of them has a different life with many responsibilities. They don't see each other much because they live apart, though still in New England. This is painful for me. It is part of my learning. I believe that as adults we create the kinds of families that we want. I feel lonely. I wish my children would reach out to me more and listen to my concerns as I reach the end of my life. However, I am humbled to remember how I did not reach out to my own parents in their elder years. The reality is that I could live another ten or even twenty years. That's a long time. In all that time, it is myself that I have to live with. I understand that letting go of expectations of my kids is the key to my health. Yet all of my four children make meaningful contact with me, in their own ways and in their own time. Occasionally they ask questions about my life grieving Kristine and listen to my responses. I find myself hesitant to share the gifts that I am experiencing, because they might not want to hear about them. They are certainly grieving their mother and might not experience any gifts at all. Certainly, if they find gifts, they'll be different from mine. Each conversation with them, however brief, is a gift to me of presence and love.

It is a gift for me to see Kristine live on in her two daughters. Kristine's blood flows in the veins of my granddaughter as well, and her facial expressions, kind gestures, and compassionate actions, not to mention her endearing cooking and household skills, live on.

All four of my kids give me, each in his or her own way, gifts from Kristine's death. Each one of them stepped up when she died.

They took on concrete tasks that I couldn't do. They each contributed to the memorial service. My daughter-in-law used her graphic design skills to produce the beautiful handout for people to take home with them. It has on it a photograph I took of Kristine when we were sailing and had anchored in a favorite peaceful Deer Isles harbor. Two daughters spoke at the service, and one daughter took special good care of Kristine's and my granddaughter. They did so while living with their own grief. As the months unfolded after Kristine died, I watched their grief produce a maturity as they developed their own healthy responses to losing their mother or stepmother. What I felt most acutely was their love. It could have gone a different way. It didn't. It went in a positive way—the way Kristine would have wanted—as we reconfigured our family without her. It went a healing way.

Two of our children were involved when Kristine and I helped start the Center for Grieving Children. They loved our tradition of concluding the center's volunteer training with pizza and were happy to help. It is a gift that the director of the center honored Kristine by giving her a memorial star on their special wall in their big family room. Though I'm an adult, I certainly felt like a child who had lost his best friend. When I walked into the center for Kristine's ceremony, I saw off to one side the door to the Volcano Room, which she and I helped institute. It's a room in which families, one or two members at a time, can express the natural anger of grief. It has padded walls, and pillows to hit and old phone books to rip up. When I felt my anger at Kristine's death, I found a rubber hose and old telephone books in my garage and brought them into my living room. I gave myself over an hour of yelling and screaming. I didn't have a choice. My anger came roaring up and out. I pounded the old phone books with the rubber hose. Elisabeth Kübler-Ross taught me well.

When Kristine's and my dear friend Bill, the center founder, was diagnosed with bowel cancer, Kristine encouraged me to spend time with him as he got sicker, even though she knew it was difficult for me. It was Kristine who told me of his death when I called her from the Philadelphia airport on my way home from work in Europe. It was Kristine who supported me when I led his memorial service in our neighborhood church. It was a generous gift that the director of the center honored Kristine with the memorial star the Thanksgiving after she died. It also gave our newly configured family a chance to gather together again and to give thanks for Kristina's life. The center's ceremony allowed Kristine's daughter to place her memorial star up next to Bill's. They were together, and I was left looking up at the two stars in gold on the wall. I keep the photo of my family at the center's memorial star ceremony on my computer desktop.

To have my children attend the ceremony and experience the gratitude the center felt for Kristine was healing. The fact that friends came was also healing for me; other people were celebrating her as well. I felt less alone.

We are now a different family, without the love and glue that Kristine provided when she was with us physically.

When our daughter and her husband endured difficult pregnancies, Kristine and I offered that love and glue for several years. The long-anticipated birth of our granddaughter was certainly a gift to us both. Now this gift is mine alone. Yet I feel as if Kristine gave me my only grandchild, my beautiful granddaughter. When the miraculous day came and we got the long-anticipated telephone call, we immediately drove down to Connecticut. New life in the family! When we walked into the hospital room, our new granddaughter was so small! Kristine noticed right away our son-in-law sat and held his new little daughter, humming a soft, loving melody to her.

Now, seeing the other end of life, I realize the suddenness of Kristine's death is a gift she gave us to spare her granddaughter and our children and friends and me a long period during which we would be forced to witness the slow, probably painful, progression of a terminal illness. We avoided watching Kristine's body shrink and become a skeleton before her eventual death.

I understand now that it is a gift to have to live by myself, alone, to refer to myself for every decision and act on it. Even as I rattle around in this old house, I smile and I cry. Without Kristine beside me here in the house, I am challenged, usually successfully, to find within myself the resources I need to live without her.

My children and siblings all watch me make this transition to living alone. They know, even with these challenges, and maybe because of them, that I love them. I know that they love me. Even as close as they are to me, I understand they know little of the gifts I am receiving.

It is a gift from Kristine that after she died our granddaughter's parents asked me to teach them meditation. I don't understand this, but it had to do with Kristine's death and me passing on to the next generation the quietude we shared, albeit separately—Kristine up in her yoga room, and me downstairs. As we talked and then meditated together, I was able to share a deeper part of myself with them than I had ever shared before.

I have occasional contact with the Center for Grieving Children and the hospice communities that remind me of Kristine. Her name is mentioned with reverence and respect. I hear gratitude for Kristine and her skills. When I enter the center, I look over and see her star on the memorial wall up next to Bill's. When I did a recent self-care workshop for their staff in the same room where Kristine supported the Wednesday-night facilitators, I felt her spirit smiling. When I help friends use hospice services, Kristine's spirit is with me.

Six

CELLAR CANDLELIGHT

Dear Jacob,

You do know that life is better with you here!! Enjoy
the colors and variety of creativity and nature!

Love, Kristine

One evening I looked out the living room window across the driveway to my uphill neighbors and saw a candle that they had placed in their cellar window. I couldn't believe it. The candlelight was just at the level of my living room window, and it clearly was a gift honoring Kristine. Every evening when it got dark, I saw the candle across the driveway just as I pulled the shades down for the night.

It is an ongoing gift from Kristine that I realize I have a lot of friends. These are neighbors as close as across my driveway, as well as others across the country and the world. My definition of "friend" has expanded. I know now that the people in my life care about me. Kristine's death has given them more permission to contact me; her quietude and shyness are no longer an impediment.

I had a legal problem come up. I wanted to turn it over to someone else to handle; I was grieving, and I did not want to be distracted. I called my neighbors next door, and they said they would talk with me the next night, for which I was very grateful. I needed help. They came over, and I explained the problem briefly. Before I finished, the attorney said, "I'll take care of it. Done. Don't worry about it. I'll handle it." This was precisely what I wanted and, even more so, what I needed. I wouldn't have any distractions from grieving Kristine. I felt lighter already and slept better. I knew that my work now was to let go of it and let my neighbor handle it. Several days went by, and I was still thinking about it, and finally I came to a stunning realization. As she had been sitting there on my couch, my attorney neighbor had been embodying the divine feminine. Though she didn't know it, the divine feminine was speaking through her and was telling me, "You will be taken care of. You have nothing to worry about. The divine feminine will take care of you." Every time I am able to remember this, I feel relieved and loved.

Because we both worked in hospice, Kristine and I talked about our own deaths and what might happen after one of us died. She said that if I died first, she would probably move to Connecticut to be close to our granddaughter. I said if she died first, I might stay

Jacob Watson

here, near my eldest daughter and the ocean. She also said she would probably not seek another partner, and she was aware I probably would.

After Kristine died, I wanted to continue my tradition of visiting my eldest daughter in Florida. Now it seemed especially important to continue this tradition, and I needed a break from being in the house without Kristine. One evening after supper in Florida, as I was feeling especially lonely staying with two couples, one person leaned forward, looked me in the eyes, and said, "Well, are you dating yet?" The question stunned me. I thought she was way off base. I muttered no in an awkward moment, but her question wouldn't go away.

Back home in Portland, my loneliness brought her question back. I know Kristine wanted me cared for if she was not here to continue as my partner. I know because she told me. I met a woman, and we had a relationship for over a year. She was the opposite of Kristine and therefore brought out another dimension of my being. It wasn't to last, but being with her gave me hope that I didn't have to be alone for the rest pf my life and provided a needed counterpoint to my grief, both of which were gifts.

Kristine was my private support for my public persona, and I counted on her for that. She knew, and I knew that she knew. Her loving support, both obvious and quiet, became newly appreciated gifts when suddenly she died and I didn't have them. When I came home late at night from teaching in Massachusetts or was away for a week staffing a Kübler-Ross workshop, Kristine always welcomed me home. These loving reunions grow in my memory and become milestones in my life—gifts to look back on and appreciate as never before.

When Kristine died, I reconnected with my first wife in Harpswell. She was loving and supportive. She called me every few weeks to check in to see how I was doing and continues to stay in touch. We often talk about our families, and the caring is evident.

It's amazing to be out and about, seeing my city with new eyes and seeing people I don't know. I want to burst outside into my street and run around waving my arms, yelling, "I see all you people connecting with each other. Don't you know Kristine died?"

I am fierce about maintaining the connections I have. When I had a massage, the practitioner pointed out to me as we started that the lamp on the table was flickering. She said it was caused by Kristine showing up with her love.

My neighbor across the street brought over some cinnamon rolls the day before Christmas. I had given them a box of kindling wood I had collected and sawed from dead branches around my proper try.

Another neighbor who had just moved in from out of state offered some consoling words and even sent me a bereavement card. A couple across the street walked over to give me a book about grief.

At our neighbor's sunrise solstice celebration, I wore the long black-and-red Irish scarf Kristine and I bought on our Ireland trip. I stepped out onto the porch and banged hard on my frame drum in the early morning chill. I walked through the intersection and down my friends' driveway to their backyard. We neighbors gathered around their outdoor fireplace and shared poems and songs. I noticed that I was the only single person present, and I felt sad. The last song the hosts played was "I'll Fly Away," and my tears came. This was the song my nieces often sang to my mother as she was dying, and they sang it again at her funeral service.

When I walked down the driveway, I could see that the brick foundation wall needed repainting. Knowing that Kristine would want me to keep the place looking nice, I felt a burst of energy to do the job. It was complex because I had to first move the gravel at the bottom of the wall so I could sand the bricks. Then I had to wipe the dust off and chip away any loose paint. I got all the materials together and started the task, beginning by the deck. I did about a quarter of it at a time. I was working my way down the driveway side on a hot day when my neighbor from across the street came over, concerned that I was getting red from the sun. She brought sunscreen and gave me some. I finished the job in a little over a month, and exulted in shoveling the gravel back up against the newly repainted wall. I felt

Kristine's approval and happiness. I appreciate these friends as never before, each one a gift in my life. The truth is that it takes time and energy to nurture these friends, and it is well worth it.

I told the owner of the local fish market that Kristine had died, and he said Kristine was one of the nicest people who came in his store. A week after Kristine died, I went to the local coffee shop, and when the owner greeted me by name and innocently asked me how I was, I told her the truth. She immediately came out from behind the counter and gave me a big hug. Then she said, "The coffee's on me." My friends confirm with their relationships with me my feeling that Kristine is now at peace, unburdened, and not in pain of any kind—none—and has no worries, physical or emotional. This is a great relief to me.

Another relief I feel comes from a recurring dream that I am sad and angry because Kristine leaves me for another man, maybe even for another family. Then, slowly, as I wake up, I remember that she has died. As awful as that is to remember, it doesn't have the sting of her leaving me for another man. It turns into a gift.

I am a member of a several communities, including those of the students and teachers at Collins Brook, the school I started in Freeport in1969, and the hospice community of southern Maine. I've been involved with hospice for many years, serving as hospice chaplain. I was part of a group that bought a building in South Portland to create a residential hospice, but it was too soon for the community, and we had to sell it. I'm part of the local counseling community. I was instrumental in creating the state rules for counselors, testifying to the regulation committee. I helped start the Center for Grieving Children. After being ordained in California, I started the interfaith Chaplaincy Institute of Maine, and I continue to support staff, graduates, and current students. When I resigned as the abbot, the school moved closer to me, settling into its new office literally one block from my house.

Kristine's death forced me to look at my life with its theme of community. Each of these places I have started, the last two with support from Kristine, have a common element. The school, the center, and the institute all provide safe places for people to come to share their natural emotions. No one is judged for having feelings in these places. In fact, people are supported and encouraged there. Their natural grief, anger, fear, and, yes, love are welcomed.

I am a member of a community of about twenty people who went on a pilgrimage to India in 2015. Reminded by regular emails from a conscientious member, we continue to meditate together on the first day of every month.

As Kristine and I had agreed before she died, I paid off two of the kids' school loans from her life insurance proceeds, sharing more gifts from Kristine.

Another dream brings a gift: Kristine and I were building an extension in a circular form onto the back of our house. We lived with the construction for a while because it was taking a long time to finish. The rooms had ample light from big windows and skylights. The feeling of the dream was hopeful and expectant. We were having a dream come true.

I had times when I thought Kristine was in the bed with me and I had to be careful not to hit her when I moved around. This feeling recurs.

An astrologer told me, "In Kristine's death, words will only go so far, perhaps at best in providing a spiritual perspective."

I can feel her spirit in her toothbrush, clothing, and shoes, which are still in their places. As I gradually put away such items, her spirit remains.

Kristine and I created the tradition of saying grace before supper, during which we each shared something we were grateful for that day. I continue this every night. I am conscious, more than ever, of taking it easy, going slowly, and feeling gratitude during the day. Kristine's absence every moment seems precious, even tangible. I remember that when I would clear the driveway and front walk of new snow, Kristine would make me fresh hot chocolate when I came inside, wet and tired. Now I make the hot chocolate for myself.

The quiet gray Maine fog reminds of the trip Kristine and I took to Ireland together. The gift was simply that we took the trip together. I can remember it as a jewel in our relationship. We loved the Celtic reminders of our shared ancestry way back in history. We weren't so far from the rolling hills dotted with stone circles demonstrating our ancestors' connection, through the land, to the gods and goddesses that they believed in.

If Kristine can leave, then everything can leave. Everything can and will leave.

It all happened the way it did. What a gift from Kristine. With her ongoing help, I remember that the universe is in charge, loving me.

One day, I sat outside on the deck in the thin sun and meditated. I heard cardinals. I allowed myself to touch my inner self and the treasures there. In the present, I saw the red male cardinal in the hemlocks in the backyard. It had not been here since Kristine's death.

Encouraged by the cardinal, I appreciate Kristine in a new way, envious of her in the way a student is envious of his teacher. Kristine is still with me spiritually. I am experiencing everyday events differently. Could it be that this beautiful day—the warm sun and blue sky—is for me? Kristine's death makes me much more conscious of how precious each moment is, a consummate gift.

When I walked the block after supper, I ran into a neighbor who teaches at the university and whose class on the natural emotions Kristine and I had taught every summer for years. Another neighbor, a woman who lost her husband two years ago, and her son stopped to say hello. I think of my many friends as I sit out on the deck and realize yet again that I am not alone. I appreciate both friends and the divine, but both imply a separation—friends in the neighborhood, the divine over there or in a church. I learn there is no separation, and with that realization comes freedom.

For months I did not want to be out in public, even if I was meeting with a caring friend. COVID-19 added to that and even gave me a great excuse to stay home. I always thought that I was—relatively speaking—the outgoing one, the extrovert, Kristine being the shy one. But suddenly I was shy. It was not that I was afraid of crying; I wasn't. Yet I wanted to be home, in the safe space I had shared for so long with Kristine.

Neighbors and friends in town and around the world remind me that as long as I am alive, I am loved. Most of them know that Kristine has died. I lose track of people, and I forget whom I've told. People forget, they move, and they die, but they are there in my life nonetheless.

The mail brings reminders of this several times a week, often when I least expect it. At first, the letters and catalogs with her name on them are pinpricks of pain—evidence that Kristine is not here anymore. Yet her name is in someone's heart or on a mailing list. Now I see that these are reminders that Kristine lives on. I open the black mailbox on the porch, and there is her name, unbidden, a friendly ghost. Now I smile, for I see that this is the way it is. Her presence still shows up on my front porch.

Seven

OCEAN CHORUS

Dear Jacob,

You have my heart. Always have, always will.

Happy day Jacob!

Anyone that knows me knows that I have salt water in my veins, and Kristine knew this from the beginning. Being a Midwesterner, it was new for her. But as she came to know me, she understood that I felt a deep communion with the ocean's salty water. I remember standing with my father in Marion when I was a little boy, looking out over the beach to the horizon. After a period of silence standing there together, I asked him what was out there, and he said "Spain." I began to understand that I could sail out there, that the sea could take me places. It was no accident that when I graduated from college I went to Spain.

I am full of gratitude that Kristine joined me in my love of sailing and the coast of Maine. I look back with a certain wistfulness on conversations that Kristine and I had. She reminded me of the recent time the two of us were sailing off Stonington and our sailboat's rudder got tangled in a lobster buoy. I got the boat hook and climbed down over the stern and tried to free us. It was no use. We were stuck fast. I didn't want to cut the lobsterman's gear. When I climbed back on board, I was exhausted. And there we were caught. I had to call the sailboat charter office to send someone out to dive overboard and untangle us. It was a humiliating reminder that I was getting older, and for safety's sake we had to rethink our vacation plans.

We gave up sailing on our own. But that salt water runs deep in my veins. I felt a need to get back out on saltwater. I proposed to Kristine that we book a passage on one of the schooners sailing out of Camden or Rockland. She lovingly but firmly said that she didn't want to go. She didn't like the small cabins and claustrophobic spaces down below or the steep, narrow ladders to get there, not to mention the inevitable close quarters with strangers. I found what I thought was a much more comfortable alternative for us. I got information about a motorized cruise. The ship was luxurious by our standards. Everything was provided for the passengers, including all meals and even an air-conditioned cabin with a conventional toilet. A positive feature was that the ship sailed from and returned to Portland; we wouldn't have to drive anywhere. The cruise route covered the waters from Portland to Bar Harbor and would visit the coastline we knew well from our sailing. It included cruising up past Georgetown and Arrowsic, old haunts of mine; through the back way to Bath; then down the Kennebec River and into the ocean; past Sequin Island; and back to Portland. But when Kristine died, our luxury cruise was never to happen.

Sequin Island was a magical place we visited on our sailing honeymoon. It was magical because it had emerged as a high fairyland out of the Maine fog. Kristine and I walked up the long wooden path to the lighthouse and looked down on our sailboat anchored in the small harbor.

Sometime in the winter, when all good sailors start planning for the summer season, it came as a gift when I realized that I could go on a schooner cruise myself and get out on the salt water. With some hesitancy, I booked a weeklong cruise for the end of June on the schooner *American Eagle*, which sails out of Rockland. Sailing my own boat at my age would have been not at all relaxing. It would have been dangerous. I tried to imagine sailing as the captain of my own boat, navigating my way from open seas into calm waters. I did not have Kristine as first mate anymore. When I reached my anchorage, it was I who was going to have to lay out the chain, prepare the anchor, choose and steer to a sheltered spot in the harbor, drop the anchor over the bow, and feed out the anchor warp. It was I alone who had the responsibility of securing the boat for the night so that I could have a worry-free sleep. No first mate anymore.

Sailing on a schooner where other people would do some of the work was a good decision. No luxury cruise for me! The schooner cruise was another gift from Kristine. When I went down below with my gear, I discovered that I was booked into cabin K—for Kristine, of course. She would not have gone on a schooner; it was perfect for me. At night I had my own small space below, and by day the sailing on the Maine coast I loved. The combination of wind and open-ocean sailing during the day, with calm protected harbors at night, nurtured my salty soul. We were a small crew of five passengers, down from the usual twenty-four, so I had plenty of space and time to myself. I imagine I was known as the quiet one. I could luxuriate in the pleasures of letting the captain navigate and steer the ship. His crew members did the sail handling and the cooking. I could enjoy being at sea.

We sailed south along the familiar coast down to a schooner festival in Boothbay Harbor. Walking around town with the other tourists, I felt alone. Everyone else seemed to be in a couple. That night after supper, I watched from the deck of the schooner as Fourth of July fireworks exploded in yellow, blue, and red splashes over the dark waters of the still harbor. As I stood there watching, each starburst felt like a tiny gift in the sky—a gift of affirmation from Kristine. I took the bursts of affirmation with me down below to cabin K.

The following day, heading back to Rockland, off Squirrel Island we sailed past a small sailboat with a young girl who was blowing soap bubbles across the water. With nothing to burst them, many made it to us. It was magical. The little girl knew her bubbles were not impeded by any obstruction and were making it across open water to us. She could see that we were enjoying them. The translucent bubbles bounced along in the southwest wind. They danced through our ropes, sails, and cabin tops, delighting us. I am reminded of the poet Rumi's wonderful line, "I didn't buy this boat to hang around a harbor."

Later that day, we were sailing out in open water miles off the coast with Vinalhaven far to windward. I was lying on the cabin top, stretched out in the sun. I began to hear a strange sound coming from the open ocean. It was a heavenly chorus of mystical female voices, a chant, sweet and melodious, coming across the water. It went on for a long time, maybe half an hour. I kept trying to make it into something or determine whether it was being caused by something, but it was true to itself, unknown and continuous, caressing me as I lay there listening. It was a profound deeply felt experience, a confirmation that the divine feminine was present for me in my life, watching over me and taking care of me.

Weeks later, full of the memories of the sandy beaches, harbor, and the bay of my childhood Marion, I was back in Portland from our annual family reunion with my three siblings, nieces, nephews, and assorted cousins. This time I was flooded with memories of Kristine's and my last visit there together. My loneliness was intense, but it was important for me to go. I was claiming Marion as my hometown. My sisters and I had a wonderful sail in the family sloop, the *Vireo*. We sailed out into the bay in the typical southwest wind, then into the cove and back around the inner harbor, duplicating Kristine's final sail the day before she died.

It is a gift that I still have access to the sea in these ways. I don't have to worry about Kristine being comfortable or adapting to seagoing ways. Kristine is now in every wind and every sea— quite a feat for a landlocked Michigander who grew up far from salt water! But she loved the coast of Maine. It was her home. And I was her mate for all those years, and now forevermore. I am filled with gratitude.

It is a gift to know that nothing could have been more fitting than for Kristine to sail by our old family property on her last sail.

Now I am sailing the rest of my life in uncharted waters. Rocks and shallows will appear. Storms and calms will happen. I only hope that with the gift of losing Kristine and the grace of spirit I will be able to navigate my way to the distant shore.

As long as I'm able, I plan to sail every summer in our family twelve-footer in Marion. It's a lovely little sailboat full of memories for me, including having a cousin teach me to sail in it. I enjoy taking some of my sister's grandchildren out sailing in what are both familiar and sacred waters to me. We always sail by the family property in East Marion. Here in Maine, I will continue to be a passenger on the wooden schooner *American Eagle* and enjoy sailing the coastal waters.

Eight

NATURAL STONE COUCH

Dear Jacob,

To welcome you home is a delight, to see the radiance of your creativity in motion is a delight. To know and experience your love is a delight!

I love you, Kristine

t is a profound gift that Kristine, without having to say so, understood my spiritual practices, which were based on meditation and gratitude. They were similar to hers. We shared the belief that spirit is everything, or everything is spirit. We each had a strong meditation practice, though we lived it in different ways. I would meditate first thing every morning, downstairs, and she would meditate in her counseling office across town.

When we first met all those years ago, we discovered that we shared the same spiritual belief systems. Our ability to love each other was based on seeing and loving each other's spirits. We understood that our counseling practices had a spiritual foundation. We knew that individuals, couples, and families who came to us were bringing us their wounded spirits.

Each of us had our own wounded spirits that we were working to heal. We were relieved and joyful to have each other as spiritual companions.

Kristine observed me closely as I expanded my spiritual practices into my daily life. They evolved into a deep awareness of my every action. How I put down a glass on the table became a spiritual act demanding an extreme focus on the present moment. All my five senses were engaged as I moved the glass down and the bottom of the glass slowly touched the surface of the table. Kristine watched and understood.

It was celebratory that while she appreciated and supported my growing spiritual practices, she allowed us to develop our own practices together. The everyday habits of living together and the quiet passion and commitment of providing a conscious home for our children expanded so that we grew together spiritually. The best example is our shared belief in the value of family meetings. This went back to my formative years when, after a conservative education, I made a hard turn left and taught in Summerhill schools. For our blended family, Kristine and I created a tradition of family meetings where we could express our feelings and make decisions. Our individual spirits began to shine through the discussions. Yes, sometimes a child stormed out of a meeting in exasperation. But the ritual of family meetings was part of our new family. More and more as we grew older, our spiritual life became the glue that held us—and our family—together.

Then, when she died, I found it useful to make rituals out of living without Kristine, just as we had made rituals out of living together. Seeing my life as composed of rituals brought me into the spiritual dimension. Ritual became a way to live the sacred in my everyday life. To do so reminded me that I was not alone. The Divine was with me.

An example of this was my choosing to walk rather than drive down to the Center for Grieving Children to deliver Kristine's memorial service donation check to the director in person. I understood that donation check in my pocket was a ritualistic way of giving energy from Kristine to the grieving families at the center.

Another example was finding two cards I had given Kristine. One thanked her for going to Ireland with me, and one celebrated her retirement from her counseling practice.

Losing Kristine in the way I did has made me more aware of how quickly a person can leave here, and the rituals that remain after he or she goes. Rituals, as Malidoma Somé reminds us, transcend space and time. So they remain after a person dies.

One such ritual was hiking with my daughter up nearby Bradbury Mountain, a favorite family trip. We climbed to the top with some of Kristine's ashes and, with a moment of silence, placed them in a small grassy space with a tiny birch tree growing out of the rock. We sat together, looking out over the tops of the trees all the way to the harbor in South Freeport.

Continuing these rituals, I went out to our favorite spot by the ocean at Cape Elizabeth, where we had discovered a natural stone couch that faced east. We had found the spot years ago and considered it our special place. It was secluded, and we loved to sit there together, knowing that just over the horizon to the east were the Maine coastal waters we sailed together.

My dreams became another form of ritual, unbidden as they were. First was the simple glad fact that Kristine was showing up in my dreams at all. I dreamed that Kristine came to me in bed and, because I was sleeping on my right side, kissed me on my left cheek. The dream gave me Kristine—now a large, all-pervading presence with me all the time, come what may. She is present without asking, everywhere, and available to me, still and forever my companion.

The Portland Valentine's Day bandit, or a neighborhood facsimile, struck—a community ritual we love, in which unknown volunteers paint big red hearts on plain white paper and paste them all over downtown. Some larger hearts appear mysteriously high up on downtown buildings. Local volunteers left a red valentine pasted on my front door. I wickedly miss Kristine on this day that celebrates love. The valentine fluttering in the wind on the front porch is a reminder of her—what I had and what I lost.

I hung in my office Kristine's family print of the ubiquitous Albrecht Durer rabbit, one that Kristine's parents had in their house by the stairs. She walked by it many times every day as a little girl, and now it graced my office wall. The rabbit sits composedly facing to the right, with its small paws together in front and its long ears poking up into the sky, now as then, a ritual across generations.

I make my life into a ritual by going slower, recognizing that every act is an event not only of this human realm but also of the spiritual realm. Every act is both of and beyond space and time. The gods are watching me, loving me as I take care of myself in this earthly life.

I have come to define practices as everything I do. When Kristine was here, I would do my yoga and meditation downstairs while I heard her doing her stretching exercises upstairs. Suddenly I understood that arranging to wake up to my Irish friend singing to me at six thirty, closing the three windows and pulling back the three shades in the bedroom, and even swinging my feet out of bed were the beginning of my daily rituals. Now I know that everything I do is a spiritual practice. This helps me lead a more conscious spiritual life. I understand now that everything I do is, as Carl Jung said, part of my myth. It's more accurate to say this than it is to judge my actions as good or bad.

This fertile and challenging myth is what Kristine left me. Now anything can happen. Anything will happen. It is my myth that I am creating.

This is a gift from Kristine that I see now with new eyes. I see with my heart now. This is a quality that Kristine has given me in her dying. It is the gift of living. I have Kristine to live with me the rest of my days.

Kristine would always bring me back to earth and remind me that people are doing the best they can. She gave me perspective and balance. She accomplished that by just being Kristine.

Kristine is with me in a new way, a way in which she can never be taken from me. She gives me this gift of the newfound time I have on my hands in her absence. I considered coming out of retirement to return to work. Perhaps I could resume seeing people for spiritual companionship. Would returning to work disturb my grieving process, and would I find the same meaning in my work? After Kristine's death, I am not sure if anything, including work, has meaning—even life itself.

When I retired, I did so largely because Kristine had retired from her counseling practice earlier that year. Both of us imagined that we would thereafter have more time to be together, and indeed grow old together. That was not to be. I found myself reflecting on what I wanted to do with the gift of freedom Kristine gave me. The answer came loud and clear: "Go back to work." I did find a new meaning in work. It was both a softer and a stronger meaning than before, and I relished it.

The teachings I gave for all those years to workshops around the country and in England and Scotland have new meaning as I apply them to myself. Finally, I am learning to accept and express my own natural emotions. I'm teaching myself to listen to my own words and to the lyrics of the songs I played.

What I have learned is that every time I experience a pang of loneliness, which is often, without fail when I express it, it kicks me into the Divine. My feelings of loneliness are because I'm a human being. With my loneliness comes the redeeming recognition that I am never alone. I am saved at the last minute by the realization that the Divine is always with me, holding me and loving me. I would not have experienced this in my life with Kristine, because I didn't need to. I had signed on to the cultural prescription pf relationships. But now, without Kristine in my life, I am forced to recognize who I really am: a divine being. Many people never get there; they are defined and encapsulated by their human existence. Kristine's sudden death propelled me into my loneliness and therefore into my divinity. I cannot just be human. Redemption and salvation are available only as a divine being. It saves me every time.

This loneliness is a gift because at the human level it is what we all are and what we will be when we die: alone, no matter how many loving family members and friends we have. We face our death, the ending of our human time, alone. Kristine's death gives me that experience every day. No one but the Divine knows who I really am. No one but the Divine knows the unfolding of my life here second by second, moment by moment, hour by hour, day by day. It is between me and the Divine. I didn't understand this until now.

I have begun to realize I can change things like what I have for lunch, how I make my bed, how I dress, and whether or not I shave or shower daily. I am sure this will continue for a while, until I am fully back in my body and attuned to what I need without Kristine, what I need as a single person. The Divine is watching.

Now I am able to live more in the present, rather than in the past as a partner to Kristine. Suddenly, as if the sun has come out from behind a bank of Maine fog, I am able to ask myself, "What do I really want?" The old automatic patterns defined by the human realm are dropping away, and more spontaneous personal and spiritual ones are taking their place. The cobwebs of my old life are blown away by a fresh wind.

Now I listen to what I want, not what Kristine and I want. It's as if I've discovered a new world, and I have a companion that will never leave me. With this new freedom, I see new possibilities everywhere.

I wrote a special issue of my *Spiritual Companionship* newsletter in honor of Kristine. I went back over photographs of her to share in the newsletter. This is my creation to express my gratitude to Kristine, and the photographs bring silence in the early quiet of the morning, along with memories and tears. Choosing and sharing the photographs gives me the ecstasy I feel when I am expressing my artistic self.

Kristine's sudden death blew my life apart. Suddenly my eyes were open wide, and I saw myself in a new way. It is a gift that I now know that I was a certain kind of person with her for those thirty-five years during which I was always in relationship with her. That meant I was a certain kind of person. That's gone. What appears before me now is the opportunity to explore a new way of being in the world. It's not that I'm a different person, but I am a different person: I could live out the expectations of a partner in a long-term relationship or not. The cobwebs linger, musty yet familiar. But it is my responsibility to take advantage of the new freedom if I want to, and if I can. Yet this is fraught with danger. On the one hand, I could content myself with the familiar ways of being with Kristine, even if she is not here, and thus I would remain trapped in an outdated pattern of living, stuck in the human realm. I could allow myself to drift aimlessly onward, lost, drifting at sea.

Or I could say to myself, "You've only got a few more years to live." I could say, "You've accomplished a lot with the schools you've started and the people you've helped. It was a good life." And it was. But it's not over. I want to live this new life without Kristine but with her gift that points beyond the human realm to the spiritual realm. Even my children, and our love, cannot fulfill my life. Thus is another gift from Kristine—and a freeing one for both my children and for me.

Every morning, I wake up alone with the challenge to live my life without Kristine. My old ways of being died with her. When I see a slice of the bright morning sun on the bedroom wall, it is a call to wake up and begin the day by myself. Kristine is not here beside me to give meaning to the new day. That is now up to me and me alone. No one, other than the Divine, cares whether I do something or not. This fact highlights the importance of everything I do being a ritual—that is, an expression of not just *the* spirit, but *my* spirit.

Nine

RED MAPLE TREE

Jacob,

This gift is for your Child within – may he always be your best friend, your most trusted confidant, and your most joyful companion.

Love, Kristine

*I*n my life with Kristine, boundaries fell away as we both experienced the oneness of our relationship. The paradox, of course, was that becoming stronger individuals created a stronger bond between us. Definite boundaries, as poet Robert Frost knew, make for a strong bond. We had our own office spaces in our house. This was originally because we both saw clients here and we wanted to be at home when the kids got out of school. It continued when the kids grew up and moved away. I had my own space, and Kristine had her own space.

That final boundary between life and death shifted before my very eyes when I experienced Kristine's death. On the other side of this boundary, she is still with me, yet in a very different form. The understanding of boundaries has transformed for me. I now see that a boundary is a veil and that there are passageways through it. As Leonard Cohen's song "Anthem" says, the cracks are where the light gets in. These are also the places where an individual's divine light may shine out into the world.

It is a gift to me that every time I open these pages to add to the gifts, in my imagination I am looking into Kristine's different-colored eyes. My favorite photograph brings her back to me. We were on one of our sailing cruises in Penobscot Bay in Maine. Kristine is at her most relaxed, away from the obligations of family, home, and her counseling practice. She is immersed in the quiet beauty of the Maine coast that she came to love. She felt at one with the peace and tranquility of the coastal waters and the sea creatures and birds. She, like me, appreciated the calm of a quiet harbor after a day spent navigating the rocky coast and trimming sails. We were together without the intrusions of the outside human world. We relaxed deeply with each other and loved to provide for our simple needs in each other's company. When we were sailing on our small boat, the boundaries melted away.

It is a gift to me that a neighbor has forced me to look at the issue of boundaries. The aging red maple tree that sits astride our boundary line has become a danger to both houses. The rugged and stately old tree provided the background for the tender photograph of Kristine and me on our wedding day. We look young, in love, and dressed up. I'm wearing a custom silk suit our kids laughingly called pajamas. Kristine is wearing the antique wedding dress she bought on impulse at an antique store in Portland's Old Port district. In the photograph, we are looking into each other's eyes, most likely contemplating the boundary between marriage and independence. Or we might just be in love!

Now I contemplate in a whole new way the boundary between life and death. Where is Kristine now? Wherever she is, she doesn't have to worry about the property line as she did while she was alive.

Newly relevant for me is the question of where I am now. Suddenly I am on one side of the boundary and Kristine is on the other. Over these months, the answer has become clear. Kristine has left this human life, yet she is still part of my life. What that means in terms of boundaries is that while she has left the human realm, I have entered more of the divine realm, where she is now. She opened the divine realm to me in a powerful way that she could not have done while still here as a human. In this way, everything now points to the divine realm. It is where Kristine lives now and where I will live soon.

As I investigate the meaning of boundaries, I ponder the instrument of cremation, the burning of Kristine's body, as a transformation from one form to another across that final boundary. Why is "cremation" spelled so much like "creation"? What if I had graduated from the University of Cremation Spirituality? Maybe I did.

I realize my two neighbors here on Glenwood Avenue have unknowingly conspired to teach me a lesson about boundaries. On one side, a neighbor is stuck in the human realm; on the other side, a neighbor transcends her boundaries to embrace the divine feminine. They have taught me that while a definite boundary is sometimes important, the ultimate boundary between life and death that I have had to explore is negligible. Boundaries are not important in the spiritual realm.

This is one land, which we learned in an instant from that iconic photograph by Neil Armstrong that he took while returning home to our planet. So, too, are life and death one. I remember the words "Eternal Life," which I painted on my ordination stole and later on my mother's casket. I have come to see that it is a manifestation of perfection that my neighbors have combined to teach me about the boundary between life and death. It looks like such a firm, unchangeable line. Here, then not here. Here, then gone. I have come to appreciate the word here.

After she died, I felt Kristine with me more at some times than at others. Did I have any say over when she was on one side, the earthly, or the other, the spiritual? What seemed so definite before didn't seem that way now, because I felt her presence with me. This usually happened late at night or in the early morning. There were times like this during the twenty-four-hour day and night, and certain times of the year, when the veil felt thinner than usual. It helped soften the veil if I simply made time to be quiet. Kristine became more available to me than I thought she was. I learned thinking doesn't help.

My aging process helps this along as I get closer to my own death. I feel less tangible, less here. I can more easily imagine this neighborhood, this community, and certainly the larger world going on without me.

When my neighbors brought this issue of boundaries into my life, it heightened my understanding of loneliness. I had to reassess my place in the world without a partner. I had no one with which to create a boundary or to talk with about boundaries in this human realm. For all of my years with Kristine, I had bought into the idea of relationship, with its boundaries coming and going. I shared my whole life with Kristine, including many thoughts and feelings every day. She knew me as no one else did, as no one else had or ever would. We talked all the time and communicated a great deal without words. It was an ongoing gift to have Kristine know me so well and respect my boundaries when necessary. I see now that this was a privilege. Not every person has the experience of being known in this way by another human being. Even in the best of relationships, a human being can't be known completely. I now understand how alone I am. The sudden removal of Kristine from my life left me a naked stranger in the universe's woods, so alone that I felt as if I were the only person on the planet. As close as we were, Kristine, while she knew me as much as any partner could, didn't really know me. This goes beyond even the existential sense of knowing—far beyond. For one thing, who I am changes every minute of my life. I experience this more than ever now, without Kristine. She provided stability, an anchor for this restless sailor. But in truth this human being is changing all the time, flooded with a cornucopia far beyond what I could share with another person, even one as loving and accepting as Kristine. I understood from this gift that only the Divine knows who I am. In this profound way, everything leads to the Divine. God knows everything about me. In my understanding, God not only loves me but also accepts me with all my human frailties.

This realization has deep meaning for me as I contemplate my own death. Kristine and I developed the confidence that we would accompany one another during our final time together. I now understand that no one, not even Kristine, can truly accompany me when I die. This is what God can do and does. This understanding brings me deep relief and satisfaction. It cements my union with God. Everything points to the Divine, the place beyond all boundaries.

The red maple tree sits on the supposed boundary line to show me that there are no boundaries, just beauty—just the Divine.

I am learning that I can take concrete steps to resolve the demands and uncertainties of the human realm. One example is contracting to have a new survey done of my boundary line with my neighbor. More importantly, in the spiritual realm I now more than ever feel the presence of Kristine, my departed friends, and my family members. They populate my life with their unique and loving presences.

I feel my three male relatives and my dear cousin who died by suicide. The fact that they are with me diminishes that hard definition of boundary between life and death, the boundary they challenged with their actions. They are all with me, even when I don't know it. We have this bond because we have the privilege of having a human birth and harvesting the lessons from our human life experience.

Ten

MAROON-AND-WHITE PAINTING

My Dear Jacob,

I smile – I melt – I love! The fullness and richness of the day with you brings me peace and calmness and joy.

The ease with which I find the me-in-you and the you-in-me tickles and delights me right down to my pinkie. I am like the bunny on the card you gave me – in ecstasy of the day we had and the joy I feel in having you in my life. I feel in wonderment at our togetherness yesterday – deeply nourished and ready to flow with my life. You are my gift that helps the pain in my life. You bring out my smiles – my lightness, my love. Thank you, my lover, my friend, my soul mate for the endearing time together!

Love, Kristine

I found that developing trust in my grief led to discovering I am not only a relationship person but also a creative one. It is my nature to create. Losing Kristine robbed me of both my primary means of loving and the confidence that I was a creative being. As I grieved Kristine, I slowly learned that these qualities, being loving and being creative, existed not only in our relationship but also in me.

It is a gift that after Kristine died, I reactivated my artistic side.

Years ago, the divine feminine was at work when I projected my writing and my painting onto two girlfriends during my Collins Brook School days. First, after not painting for several years, I admired a woman's paintings, first in Maine, then in Greenwich Village. She used huge canvases, bright colors, and abstract shapes. I was mystified by her creative spirit but entranced by it as well. I went to New York and was envious of her huge Greenwich Village gallery space, devoted to painting, with stacked canvases, brushes, and paint tubes scattered around. I loved the deep, rich smell of her paints. I admired that her tiny living space was tucked as an afterthought in her painting studio.

After writing a novel a few years earlier, I poured my daily feelings into pages and pages of yellow legal paper and stuffed them into envelopes to send off to the second woman, who worked as an editor for a major magazine in Chicago. We traded reams of paper for almost a year. When the thick envelopes stopped arriving in the mail, I knew the relationship was over.

Propelled by Kristine's death, I am owning my projections and developing my own artistic creativity through both painting and writing.

The first artwork is a maroon-and-white painting that I made over fifty years ago when I was a freshman in college. I found it up in the garage covered with dust. It was in serious need of cleaning. I wiped it carefully and sprayed it with a fixative to brighten it up and protect the old oil paint. I hung it in my office opposite the big couch where my Spiritual Companionship clients sit. Some of them remark on it, and if appropriate, I tell them the story. It is an abstract work, so the viewer can make of it what is significant to him or her, and many do.

The second artwork is a photograph I took on a trip to the Bahamas. I was using a 35mm camera then and took the photograph in an open-air market. The subject, a Black woman, was shopping and did not see me take the picture across several aisles of vegetables.

The third, more recent, piece is the silk stole I made for my interfaith ministry graduation in California. Our small class went out to a silk artist's studio for the day to make our ceremonial stoles we would wear for our graduation ceremony. We each designed a stole bearing the motto of the seminary: "Art is prayer made visible, music is prayer made audible, dance is prayer embodied but the greatest art we practice is the art of compassion which is art in action and service." I had put the stole away on a hanger in the downstairs closet and took it out to wear only when I performed weddings, funerals, and other ceremonies. Yet, as I told my chaplaincy students, chaplaincy is not something you do; it is who you are. Encouraged by a friend, I brought my stole out of the closet. I understood what I was doing, benefitting from the idea of "out of the closet." Instead of being hidden among winter coats and sailing jackets, it now graces my office space, draped so the messages can be seen. The words "Eternal Life," which came to me while I was painting the silk, stand out.

The words have a new meaning now.

My pieces of art are out of hiding now, displayed front and center where my friends and clients can see them. I see them first thing every morning when I come down to meditate, and every time I step into my space. I have moved some of my art supplies from the basement up into my office, bringing them up into the light, where I can use them every day.

Artist friends that knew Kristine continue to be a part of my life and therefore bring her into my life every time I see them and think of them. Sometimes they ask me about her and want to know more about her and about our relationship. Early on in my grieving, I didn't like this, but now I like it a lot. It is a way that Kristine continues to live on in my life, and be a part of it in the present moment.

I've been influenced by well-known people, most of whom Kristine knew because of me—people who impacted both of us. I remember times when Kristine and I would take a visiting teacher out for dinner, and I would feel like a fly on the wall. The well-known teacher and Kristine had a bond beyond me. All I could do was watch. Now when I encounter them in person or in their books, Kristine comes with them.

Eleven

LOVE CARDS

Dear Jacob,

I honor all that is important to you and that healthiness inside and around you. May you have more of that peace this year. This gift is only a token of the passionate expressions of being that I associate with you!

I love you, Kristine

This is the chapter that could have Kristine's name in the title. But her name isn't there. It is a gift, though hard won, that I can no longer rely on Kristine. The ways in which I saw myself and led my life in the reflection of Kristine I cannot do any longer. I must own up to the fact that it is my life and no one else's. I am a partner only with the Divine. Kristine is now part of my Divine life. While I still feel that she is supporting me and is forever on my side, I must now expand to fill all the corners of my life without her. I cannot rest on her or count on her to fill in my holes, to catch me when I fall, to remind me of who I am. It is now up to me. It is the ultimate gift. It is a gift, if they choose to embrace it, that most people experience when they lose a loved one or when they themselves are dying.

My gifts of grief keep unfolding and will continue to do so as long as I'm alive. They will flow to our four children, as long as they are alive, when they are open to receiving them. While some gifts will be obvious to them, some will be unexpected and therefore all the more powerful. The way that her love continues to flow to me, my children, and the larger world is Kristine's legacy.

In over thirty-five years of being together, Kristine and I exchanged many cards. My tears come when I find them in drawers and manila files, and see them on bookshelves. I reread them often. The cards reflect both the traditional holidays as well as our own family milestones. They express the deep love Kristine and I felt toward each other.

I know that if my office caught fire again, these love cards would be the first things I'd grab on the way out the door. While the words are burned into my heart, the artwork and photographs, some of which were created by people we know, are just as stunning. They reflect Kristine's love of birch trees and our mutual love of sandy beaches, blue skies, and sailing the Maine coast.

It is a gift that all of the experiences of living with Kristine are forever mine. The bad things are in the past, never to be repeated. The good things are likewise in the past, except these can be recalled in my memory. This brings me into the present, because these judgments of good and bad are themselves forever changed. I realize that judgments like "good" and "bad" are only superfluous, superficial judgments. The Divine has a way of leveling them out to be simply experiences. What is bad one day could be good the next. What is good one day could be bad the next. It doesn't matter. What matters is love. I loved Kristine, and she loved me. This understanding propels me even further into the spiritual realm.

It is a paradox that accepting these gifts from Kristine makes my life lonelier. There is now no excuse. I am left on my own. Then the flash of lightning comes. The only solace is that provided by the spiritual realm. It is the most transformative surprise of all. Now I am not only without Kristine; I am without anybody. This is now acceptable to me. It is even preferred, because now I have nothing to lose. It is as if I have graduated from this human school, except I know I have more to learn; otherwise, I wouldn't be here.

Looking ahead, I am painfully aware that Kristine is gone and will not be able to share with me a host of family anniversaries, births, deaths, birthdays, holidays, and graduations. I will receive no more cards from her. She will miss our professional milestones—for example, the thirty-fifth anniversary of the founding of the Center for Grieving Children, which we both helped start. Yet those milestones, professional and family, will still occur—another gift.

It is a gift to know that anything that happens now in my life can't be worse than Kristine dying suddenly, meaning that everything seems more manageable than it otherwise might.

It is a gift that Kristine's and my relationship was up to date. We were current with each other; there was no important information that we hadn't shared with each other. Kristine knew that I loved her, and I knew that she loved me. There is no greater gift in a relationship. What that means is that I will have Kristine's love forever. She has my love forever. To be clear, being up to date, while helpful, did not mitigate the shock of her sudden heart attack and death.

It is a gift to know that Kristine will never leave me; I will never leave her. Yes, this is an odd thing to say about somebody who has died. But it speaks to the revelations I am experiencing.

The biggest gift is that Kristine's love for me encourages me to take care of myself as she would take care of me. I don't hear her voice, but I feel her presence, which will always be with me as a loving spiritual companion.

I imagine the stark fact that living in my house, as much as I want to continue that, is a waste of resources, as well as perhaps too much responsibility for an aging man like me. I am plagued by guilt every time I drive downtown and see a homeless encampment. I have yet to make peace with this discrepancy.

I know I will have continuing losses as I get older. Some will be my capabilities as a physical being, and others will be because I will lose family members and friends. In this human realm, I am now more accustomed to grief—or, as Handel said, I am acquainted with grief. All these years later, what a client said of me has become personal: "He's a grief guru."

Kristine will continue to show up in my dreams, as well as in the photograph albums and computer photographs, forever.

From now on, she will be wearing her signature orange sun visor and orange shirt, sitting on the family float in Marion, right in the middle of the Watson matriarchs.

Kristine is standing on the dock, saying to me, and only me, "I'm done. I've done all I can do. You're on your own. I send you off on your final journey with as many gifts as I can. May you harvest my gifts and use them to create your own as you sail into your own uncharted waters, as I have into mine. May you have a glorious sail, just as I've had with you. I have full confidence in you. I know you will have a wonderful sail."

Twelve

LONELY SAILOR

*T*his is where a card from Kristine should be. But there are no more cards. I won't find any more cards on the dining room table, on my desk, in the mail, or tucked under my pillow. I will receive no more cards from Kristine. From now on, this is my path alone.

Whatever gifts I was given are part of me now. They do keep coming to comfort and change me. The journey now, however described in my hopeful sailing metaphors, is mine and mine alone.

This last chapter is about gifts of grief going forward. After all, this grief is part of my lifelong grief. I felt grief early on when my three younger sisters and brother never seemed to have to go through the same experiences and time frame that I did as the eldest son. They seemed to get important things like bicycles and books about sex at a much younger age than I did.

I felt grief from being rejected by Harvard University, the school that accepted my father, uncles, and cousins. It was a grief to have my Collins Brook School close. It was a grief to have my first marriage end. I felt much grief when a number of close male friends died. It was a grief to have my father die. It was a further grief to have my mother die. Losing Kristine is the biggest grief I have ever felt. It is a further, ongoing, grief to let go of my expectations of my children. They are beautiful, wonderful people in their own right. It is my work to let go of how I'd like them to be. This, letting go, is a common task of any parent.

It is a gift to have experienced my journal getting me through the first year of grief at losing Kristine. Fortunately, because I'm a writer, the journaling came as a matter of course, something that I did every day. I still have to remember to give my grief its acknowledgment and expression. For me, writing is only the first step.

It is a gift to be reassured that what I've been teaching others for years is absolutely true. Acknowledging and expressing natural emotions does open a path to the spiritual realm. The title of my book *The Emotional Path to Spirit* is an accurate one. I have learned this truth as never before. It is as if the ideas were just ideas; now I know them in my soul. Through this grief, my soul has grown to a new level.

Elisabeth Kübler-Ross knew what she was doing when she designed her five-day Life, Death, and Transition workshops to focus on the acknowledgment and expression of the natural emotions for three days and part of the nights. Workshop participants had the experience of expressing the natural emotions of their stories in the nonjudgmental presence of strangers. Once workshop participants had that transformative experience, they could trust their feelings in a new way. Many would return to future workshops or find ways back at home to express their natural feelings. Once that was done in a workshop, or at least begun, the emphasis turned to the spiritual, to the Divine. Walking into the meeting room that fourth day was like walking into a cathedral. When natural emotions, such as grief, are expressed safely, they open new pathways to the spiritual realm.

It is a gift to me that I can now accept what Ken Wilber calls being a "divine schizophrenic." What are labeled the best and the worst experiences of our lives often happen at the same time. Though I get caught in the contradictions of being human and the typical characteristic of judging everything to be either good or bad, I now live more in the everlasting presence, where everything is exactly as it should be. Sometimes I like it, and sometimes I don't like it, but it is how it is as a human.

It is a gift to lose some of my rigidity, to let go of my automatic reflexes, and to know what I want. Contrary to my expectations, no one around seems to notice the difference. I now feel more spontaneous and more in tune with each moment than ever before. It is this gift that finally made me grow up. I don't have any excuses anymore. All the faults are mine. They welcome me into the spiritual realm.

It is a gift to move into my retirement as a "re-firement," to use Matthew Fox's word.

It is a gift that my meditation often brings to my awareness family and friends who have died. This reminds me that they are still a part of my life and that they watch over me and celebrate me. I feel their presence every day. I am grateful they know that I am still here in the human realm and therefore need their ongoing support to complete the work I have yet to do.

It is a gift to know that the Divine Feminine, as I learned from my lawyer neighbor, will always take care of me. I just have to remember that.

It is a gift that I am taking care of myself physically as well as emotionally. I realize now that my grief literally weighed me down. I am recovering from walking with a stoop, leaning forward. I'm back to exercising.

I still feel my loneliness as my life goes forward; I am alone to contemplate the end of my life. I have a new sensitivity and appreciation for the solitude of my life, the solitude of every life, particularly when facing death.

I feel that the greatest gift is one that encompasses everything. I understand as never before that I am alone with the Divine and am therefore never alone. I have realized that it is fine that I'm alone. It is fine that I am living my life as best as I can, in all the ways that I want to. I am full of love, and I give to everyone what I can to the best of my ability. I answer to no one but the Divine. Few humans know this truth about me, or at least that's what I perceive.

I try to live every detail of my life as consciously as possible. I now know that this consciousness means that I feel all the natural emotions exquisitely and deeply, indeed, as never before—certainly not before Kristine died. I learn over and over that these feelings simply want acceptance and expression. That makes me both very special and very ordinary. Right now, I feel very ordinary. I say, "Don't wait. Join me to inhabit life as fully as we know how."

This is where I say something about g gifts going forward. But there is no going forward, just as there is no living in the past. The present moment is our only gift. Just as there are all these gifts from grief, so are there gifts from every experience. Life itself is a gift.

Afterword

None of these gifts would have been given to me had Kristine not died but lived. They are set in the context of Kristine's death. Yet they shine forth. I cannot explain how many precious and wonderful events happened because a disastrous one happened. I have harvested these gifts from a brutal event. I don't know how I could have done otherwise. I know that these gifts allowed me to survive.

Because other people seem to be interested in my revelations, I can do more than survive. I now have the privilege of sharing the gifts I am receiving by writing this book. I also have opportunities to give workshops with the title Gifts of Grief.

I know that I am fortunate to have these gifts. Not everyone does. Not everyone will. I also know that allowing myself to acknowledge and express my natural emotions allowed me to harvest these gifts. The emotions come first by necessity. It is only then that the gifts can come, with their spiritual essence. It is the spirit that survives. Kristine's spirit is alive and well in my heart and in the hearts of those who loved her, particularly her family. I hope this book will share Kristine's spirit beyond these circles.

I have slowly developed the assurance that precious gifts will continue for the rest of my life and beyond. The momentum of my life is cheered on by Kristine. She is still alive and applauding my every action. She knew me well and she knows me well. She loved me and who I was, and she loves who I am today. It is unexpected and extraordinary for me to experience such affirmation and aliveness—especially from someone who is supposedly dead.

Kristine has never been more alive for me; that is how close we are now and forever.

Kristine caresses me all the time. This morning I felt her loving fingers move through my white hair, reminding me again that she is always with me.

Acknowledgments

I am grateful for the encouragement of my family and friends, especially the following:

Lea Watson
Joe Wolfberg
Eva Goetz
Nancy Mullins
Mike Miles
Elizabeth Peterson

About the Author

Jacob Watson grew up in a New England family, attended traditional schools, then took a hard turn left. He founded Collins Brook School, an alternative Summerhill day and boarding school, then became a grief counselor. He helped start the AIDS Project in Portland. He was a senior staff member of the Elisabeth Kübler-Ross Center, leading Life, Death, and Transition workshops nationally and overseas. Jacob helped start the Center for Grieving Children, where he has trained volunteer facilitators for thirty years.

He was a hospice volunteer, chaplain, board member, trainer, and supervisor.

The broken hearts and wounded spirits of his clients—and a fire that damaged his counseling office—propelled him into ministry.

Jacob graduated in creative writing from the University of Pennsylvania, received an MA degree in humanistic counseling from Beacon College, and received a doctor of ministry degree from the University of Creation Spirituality. He was ordained an interfaith minister by the Chaplaincy Institute of Arts and Healing Ministry.

He is the founding abbot of the Chaplaincy Institute of Maine and devotes his life to teaching, writing, and prayer.

Jacob's teachings, meditations, and children's stories are available on the free phone app Insight Timer.

He offers workshops for groups and individual spiritual companionship, and is available at revjwat@gmail.com and 207-761-2522. He also has a website at revjacobwatson.com.

Printed in the United States
by Baker & Taylor Publisher Services